Baarish

Ke

Saath

A NOVEL BY SHALINI JOSE

Dear Travis,

Thank you for supporting my book and its
Cause – I truly appreciate it! ♡

With a ton of love,

Shalini Jose

The story, names, characters, and incidents portrayed in this novel are fictitious. Apart from the brief mention of some well-known public figures and popular media, no identification with actual persons, whether they are living or deceased, places, buildings, and products is intended or should be inferred. Any similarity to any person living or dead is purely coincidental.

This story contains elements of violence and sexual abuse. Reader discretion is advised.

Have any questions or feedback?

Email shalinijosenovels@gmail.com

Sometimes, there are moments in life that just happen.

Moments so unforgettable...moments so impactful...that they

leave a story to be told.

Chapter 1

Zindagi would always tell me that with the rain, there was a sign from God. This particular evening, I was frustrated in trying to understand what God was trying to tell me. I had just had a horrific day and was now just driving...driving as far as I could to get my mind off everything that had happened...to get rid of the pain.

Just two nights ago, my best friend Nima had suddenly gone missing. Immediately, our team went out searching for her and this morning, we found her...

Completely unconscious, she was found on the fourth floor of an abandoned building just a stone's throw away from the police station. We found her...but at the same time, felt like we had still lost her. It didn't seem like she could make it, but all my heart wanted to do was to believe that she could.

I couldn't get rid of the image of her in that building from this morning. She had been brutally raped and shot in the

7

chest. She had been thrashed against that dirty pavement, her body bruised and beaten. Stab wounds covered her chest, stomach, and legs, and a pool of her own blood rested beneath her. Not even monsters are treated with such brutality.

We soon rushed Nima to the hospital, where she had just begun to slightly stabilize. The doctor even said that it was a miracle that Nima wasn't brain dead after receiving such serious blows to the head, although the extent of rehabilitation she would need could not be known until she woke up. My fellow officers and I could do nothing but watch as the doctors and nurses rushed to treat Nima's wounds and stop her blood loss.

After a few seconds, one of the nurses told us that we needed to shift over to the waiting room, so we moved towards that direction while trying to keep our eyes on what was going on with Nima for as long as we could. Once she was out of sight, I decided to grab a cup of coffee and tried to stay awake for a bit longer to see if there was any progress. My hopeful thoughts wrestled with my negative ones.

"Need any sugar baby?" asked Arman with a voice that attempted to seem soothing and vulgar at the very same time.

I knew that he was the one responsible for all of this. I had no doubt that it was him. But somehow, he always managed to have any bit of evidence against him destroyed. Always. My blood boiled in silence.

"What's wrong? Not feeling so good today?" he chuckled.

I turned away from him and continued making my coffee.

"Don't ignore me...you know you shouldn't ignore me baby. You remember don't you...I know you do," he whispered.

I do remember. Two years ago, he introduced himself to me as the head officer of our department and with aggressive strength in his grip, shook my hand. He was an extremely well-respected man in our community, and to this very moment, he holds that same, powerful, disgusting respect.

It was clear that he wore his uniform with great confidence, and the medallions sewn on his shirt reflected his pride.

Within a few seconds of meeting me, I remember how he handed me a new uniform and a key for my locker and then wished me well for my future as part of the department. Disgustingly, I still recall how, in those first few moments, I felt that he seemed friendly and welcoming, genuine and even charming.

A few days later, Arman came up to my desk and began flirting with me, which I had been told to be cautious of by some of my fellow female officers. He asked for my phone number, and when I declined, he just laughed and then walked off. From that day forward, he would lean up on my desk, stroke my back, and lick his lips as he eyed me top to bottom. No sense of respect. No sense of shame.

As a head officer with access to my application files, he was able to get my number and began to call me sporadically, oftentimes drunk and in the middle of the night, pushing for sex and doing so in such an aggressively vulgar way. I filed a harassment case, but my case was dropped almost immediately. I was told that Arman was just being silly. And that boys will be boys.

After that, I tried to bring it up to a different department, but everything I said was ignored as pettiness. Even some of the women could not see the problem.

"It's just something you have to get adjusted to, which will come with time," they would say.

"Are you sure that you're not luring him in?" others would ask.

I could do nothing else but try to ignore him *and* them. But the more I ignored him, the more aggressive he became.

Just a couple of days after my initial case was dropped, I remember standing alone in the breakroom as I was closing up my locker. Only the sound of the air from the AC system was audible. I had a picture of me and Nima in our uniforms hung up in the locker. No medals, no status, but still so much pride in what that uniform meant. Now, I ask myself if any of that means anything at all.

I remember how fixated my thoughts were on the idea that Arman's behavior was being passed off as nothing while I was standing in that locker room. I was so consumed by the anger towards the reality of so much ignorance. But before I could even begin to process that anger, Arman came up behind me and pushed my back against the lockers with an intense forcefulness, pressing his cold hand against my mouth. I remember suddenly feeling a blade at my neck.

"You shouldn't ignore me Mandira. I don't like to be ignored," he said as he lightly pressed the blade against my skin. He grinned crudely as he ran his fingers through my shirt and stroked my breasts. I remember struggling beneath his grip.

"Was there really a need for the harassment case? I don't think it's harassment or abuse, especially if your body consents to it...and enjoys it."

He tugged at my belt, and within seconds, he took pleasure in my new fear of him...my subordination to him...as his fingers pressed inside of me. I don't even remember what he said to me in those moments...I was just so scared.

After a few minutes, he let go of me and slammed the locker door behind me with a smirk in his eyes. As he walked off, I remember standing frozen in that locker room for at least twenty minutes. All I could feel was the pounding of my heart through my ears. As I stood in that empty room, my heart was shattered, my thoughts broken.

I could not keep my emotions contained. I was frustrated and scared and angry and terrified. But, again, I was simply told to get over it. I tried speaking to higher officials, but my complaints remained filed in several layers of paperwork without any solution.

Many officials actually told me to leave the job if I felt like I had been violated. As much as that suggestion infuriated me, I really did consider leaving. But in my mind, I couldn't accept the idea of allowing someone like Arman to control me and shape my life. I decided to stay and continue working through the police force, especially because I wanted to fix the corruption that had become so routine within the system - a system that was meant to protect the same kinds of victims.

As I made my way up the department ladder, I realized that I wasn't the only one who had experienced such assault. I wasn't the only one to have been silenced despite the earnest calls for help. So many other officers told me about Arman's sexual behavior, but many of them could not afford to complain to officials, who, along with the rest of the community, all looked to Arman with much prestige and respect.

He was secretly known only by his victims for abusing women and sexual harassment. The problem is that the system is so corrupt that all the evidence simply gets put under the table or put in the wrong hands, especially because of Arman's high status in the department and in the community.

Social condemnation and judgment were among the other risks many women did not want to take. Men's sexual hunger is celebrated...despite the means of satiation. Women, on the other hand, are chastised for any hint of sexuality,

now to look at him. To even have him anywhere in my thoughts. I was frustrated. I was weak.

***

Walking through the third floor of the hospital, I looked at each door that held a patient behind it, thinking about all the different situations different people faced. This floor was specifically for patients who had been physically and sexually abused and were in need of medical care as a result. There were boys and girls, men and women who became patients on this floor every day. Many of their stories destroyed, forgotten, or hidden.

Soon, I reached Nima's room and looked at her resting unconsciously in the hospital bed. It had been a few hours since she had been out of surgery, but she looked just like she had when I first saw her in that building.

Why her? Why anyone? Nima supported me throughout my entire effort to get Arman to be held responsible for all that he had done. The day Arman assaulted me, she was the first person I told, and she was the first person to take a

19

stand for me after seeing the toll he took on me. I could not help but think of her last words about the situations involving Arman before she too went suddenly and completely silent about him.

"I always thought that it would be so much easier to bring these assaults to the attention of people who could bring true justice for the victims," she would say. "But what happens when the people you count on for justice don't believe in justice at all? The victims are forced to keep quiet and for those who take the risk and file the complaints, their words are just passed off by the courts as nothing. When will it become something to them? We can't stay quiet about this...we just can't."

A few more hours after Nima had gotten out of surgery, her family had arrived - her mother, Shahida Aunty, and younger sister, Nisha. As time slowly passed, the situation seemed to gradually get just a bit better...Nima was stabilizing, her family was there, and the doctor continually mentioned that we had less to worry about than initially expected because of the fortunate positioning of all of Nima's stab wounds. But Nima's mom and Nisha had sorrowed looks, and the news from the doctor did nothing to ease the pain on their faces. It was like taking a single drop of water from a devastating flood.

Shahida Aunty was a very sweet woman - always with a smile on her face and always filled with so much hope and positivity. She was famous in our town for her homemade kulfi, which she made fresh daily from the mangos in her own backyard. All the children in the town would come to her doorstep every day after school, and with a huge smile on her face, she'd pass around steel cups of her amazing kulfi. I can still hear the clanking of our empty steel cups after our bellies were full from that famous kulfi. Shahida Aunty loved to make other people smile, and it was easy because her smile was always so contagious. Today was the first time I had ever seen her without her smile.

Nisha, Nima's sister, was just like her mother. Always so happy and positive. She had the same wavy black hair tucked under a hijab, hazel eyes, and wonderful personality that Nima had. There was a seven-year age difference between Nima and Nisha, but from their relationship, it always seemed like they had been with each other from the very beginning. Never have I seen a bond between sisters so strong. Nisha always had this sparkle of joy in her eyes. Today, that was replaced by a look of helplessness.

Both of them looked immensely tired, but they held on to Nima with every bit of energy they had left within them. Their gaze never left Nima and within their gaze, there was immense hope. The hope that Nima would speak to them again, the hope that Nima would remember who they were, the hope that their lives could somehow return to normal. Shahida Aunty had even brought a large jug of her fresh kulfi with the hope that she could treat her daughter to her favorite dessert again...to ease Nima's pain slightly with the joy the kulfi always brought to her.

Shahida Aunty always held on to the belief that people must never lose hope - it's an attitude I've learned from her and continue to hold on to as well. It's the hope that they had that brings tears to my eyes right now - that makes me realize how we truly never know what the future can bring, despite the hope and confirmation we receive.

***

Around 6 p.m., I had decided to go pick up some food for Nima's family from the small food stand just outside the hospital. The hospital itself was charity-based and was one that I visited often. It was a small, peach colored four story building that could hold about 20 patients on each floor and staffed just over 40 employees in addition to the many volunteers.

For the last six years, I've worked as a volunteer educator and support system at the hospital for children who have been abused. Every free moment I get, I'm at this hospital. The kids that enter these doors every single day mean the world to me. The people I meet here, the stories I hear, the experiences I've had...nothing cuts me with reality like this hospital does.

I remember working here on my first day. Within the first ten minutes of stepping foot into this hospital, a seven-year-old girl who had been sold into sexual slavery was brought in. The young woman who had found her lying in the streets didn't know it, but that beautiful seven-year-old girl was already dead. The little girl had been so brutally beaten and repeatedly raped. We soon realized that many of her organs were gone too - most likely for sale on the black market. Crinkled newspaper replaced her heart, kidneys, and liver. We didn't even know her name...a moment that taught me just how fragile life can be.

All the officers had returned to work or gone back home. It had been almost fourteen hours since we brought Nima to the hospital and around seven hours since Nima's family had remained at her bedside. Nima had woken up momentarily, only to go into a deep sleep again a few minutes later. Her family had not eaten all day, and the sounds of their growling stomachs were the only things that broke the sound of silence and tears.

The chaat house outside was where I would usually take kids for their first true meal, as many of them had been rescued from the sex trade and abusive homes that kept them starved. As simple and cheap as the food stand was, the food from there was always the confirmation for them that they were now truly safe and protected.

As I was waiting for the food for Nima's family, I ran into Jamal, my brother and another best friend. He volunteered as a part-time teacher and also volunteered with me at the hospital, along with his wife, Simran. He too was an officer but worked in a different branch, splitting his time between Kerala and Mumbai to focus on organized political crime and terrorism. He was always someone who could brighten my day, even during the worst of storms.

"Hey Mandira...how's Nima doing?"

"The doctor says she feels like Nima is going to survive...I hope so. She opened her eyes for a little bit. Seemed slightly aware of what was going on," I said as I thought about the words Nima kept on repeating when she

25

regained some of her consciousness. But before I could say anything about it, I noticed tension in Jamal's posture.

"What's wrong?" I asked with concern.

"Mandira - the evidence from the scene this morning was tampered with. It's no longer admissible in court."

"It doesn't surprise me. How much is it Uncle?"

"One hundred rupees beta," said the vendor as he threw a small white towel over his shoulder.

As I reached into my pocket for cash, I could see that Jamal was surprised by my lack of surprise. "You remember when we were kids, Zindagi would always check under our beds and in our closets to make sure there were no monsters, especially after we watched those scary movies, even though she told us we probably shouldn't."

"Yeah," said Jamal. "I still remember you climbing into my bed after watching that exorcist movie. You would say you thought you saw a monster in your closet, but with the lights on, it was only a rack of clothes." He smiled lightly at the memory while his sternness in the seriousness of the situation remained.

"Yeah," I slightly smiled back. "Now I feel like monsters are real...and still, no one can see them."

"We'll find justice for Nima. I promise you we will," he said as he gently put his hand around my shoulder. "It's just going to take some time."

"How much more time Jamal? You and I both know that this is going to keep happening...Arman abuses a woman, literally pays for his actions, and repeats the cycle. We know how many pieces of evidence go unchecked, how many rape kits go untested and thrown out. How many more times are they going to let him pass by...those women aren't numbers...Reina, Neha, Madhuri, and now he's taken someone else's life and that's being totally ignored. How many women does it take for people to see Arman?" I said, raising my hands in frustration.

"What's happening to people Jamal? Even I feel like this is becoming a normal thing...and it's making me sick...the fact that this is slowly becoming a normalized part of life for people."

The anger in my voice grew.

"I'm sorry Jamal...I'm not angry with you...it's just so frustrating. If direct recordings of him abusing women isn't enough, what is?"

"Give me your hand Mandira," he said as he put his other hand out for me to hold.

As I gave him my hand, he looked me in the eyes and said, "I promise you Mandira - we're going to get Nima justice for this. I have no doubt that you'll make sure of it."

I exhaled heavily as I looked towards the ground.

"Have you seen Jagan anywhere?" I asked. "The last I saw him was this morning at the scene. Krish and Aamir had to pull him away from Nima because he was so distraught and wouldn't let go of her - I'm worried about him."

Jagan was Nima's fiancé. A gentleman and sweetheart who matched Nima's personality perfectly. They were set to get married two weeks from today.

"I just saw him go into the hospital," said Jamal as he turned his face towards the main entrance of the hospital. "He was bringing in some clean clothes for her and a bouquet of flowers. I think he'll be spending the night here with her."

"I'll have Nima's family stay at my place tonight. Since she's in intensive care, they won't allow more than one person to be with her."

"Beta - food's ready," said the vendor in a gentle voice hoping to not interrupt our conversation.

"Thank you Uncle."

Just as I was about to pick up the food, I noticed a teenage boy acting somewhat strange at the entrance of the hospital. He was wearing blue jeans and a bulky black jacket - it seemed very out of place for the hot and humid weather. Pacing back and forth, he was continuously observing his surroundings. Jamal, noticing that my attention had suddenly shifted, moved his attention towards the direction of the boy that I was staring at.

"Jamal, does he seem a bit suspicious to you?" I asked as I kept my eyes locked on the boy.

"Who are you talking about Mandira?" asked Jamal as he turned to see who I was looking at.

"The one in the black jacket and ripped blue je-"

The boy suddenly made eye contact with me and then ran into the hospital through a side entrance. I ran after him...something was wrong.

Jamal ran after me, calling out my name and trying to figure out what I had seen.

I ran to the entrance, about 50 meters away from the door, when I saw him - that boy with the black jacket and ripped blue jeans - perhaps eighteen or nineteen years old. He was sweating, had a scar that ran below his right eye, and was holding a small liquor bottle in his hand. He was shaking and looked scared. There was uncertainty in his eyes. And within seconds, he pulled off his jacket. He was a suicide bomber.

My instincts told me I had to stop him - those people in the hospital would die. But before I ran even a couple of steps,

Jamal grabbed a hold of me and held me back - he knew that I wouldn't make it in time and that I too would die if I came any closer to the building.

I fell to my knees and began to cry hysterically as Jamal held me back. In a fourth of a second, the entire building exploded in flames...a domino effect. Bombs detonated up the hospital. All four stories...over 100 people. For a moment I stared...for that one moment I stared at that building hearing nothing but the flames and seeing nothing but bloody orange. And like that, Nima was gone. Her family...gone. Every person in that hospital...each nurse...each doctor...each patient...each loved one...each bit of hope...gone. After that, I could do nothing but cry in Jamal's arms.

***

The rain amidst my drive this evening seemed to capture my emotions - heavy and raging. My mind was in shock. My thoughts completely broken. I couldn't cry physically anymore, but my mind was flooded in tears.

I was driving nowhere around 1 a.m. in the heavy rain. I had been on the road for more than five hours - I just wanted to get my mind somewhere else. I was continually thinking in circles...questioning myself about anything that could have been done to prevent what had happened...thinking about the hope that had been alive just a few hours ago.

I couldn't take my mind off what had happened to Nima. It was just two days ago that we had sat down for lunch at Lakshmi Bhavan with our favorite meal - ghee roast finished off with a cup of Bru coffee. Everything happened so fast...everything was gone so fast.

A worse storm was coming, which was becoming more evident with the growing sound of thunder and increasing winds. It became more and more difficult to drive, so I decided to slow down a bit, but continued driving. I didn't mind being stuck in the rain in such an isolated area - it would give my mind something else to focus on. My mind kept telling me that I was done...too exhausted to keep on dealing with the pain.

Soon, I turned down my radio. I had been listening to some old Hindi songs for the last few hours, but I finally thought I would try to reflect on everything that had happened in silence. This entire drive had been about pushing the pain away, but I realized that the pain wouldn't go away until I dealt with it. And it was much harder than I thought. I couldn't take the silence - the pain was so loud. I turned the radio back on again.

A few minutes later, I couldn't see anything clearly anymore through the windshield. Rain was falling like it never had before. Life felt quiet. Lonely. Difficult.

But suddenly, something on the side of the road caught my attention.

Just ahead, I could see some rain bouncing off something. As I drove closer, it looked like someone was lying flat on the ground. There was no movement at all, besides the heavy rain that bounced off what looked like a dead body. I stopped my car and tried to get a closer look at what had happened.

As soon as I opened my door, the sound of the rain tripled. I ran out into the rain and knelt beside the person who had been lying there.

He was a built man with a full, clean-cut beard and looked about my age, but a little older. What stood out to me the most, however, were the beatings that he had received on his body. His body was bruised everywhere, and he had stab wounds across his chest and legs. His clothes were torn and whatever clothes remained on him stuck to his body because of his blood. Beneath him, there was a pool of blood mixed with the fresh rain water.

I checked for his pulse, and it was there. His heart was racing. I needed to get him help, but the nearest hospital was more than a three-hour drive from where I was. He would not last that long - he had already lost too much blood. My mind began racing to retrace where I was...thinking about my drive here...people I might have seen...places I might have passed...trying to think of someone or something that could help this man. I had blanked out the entire drive - my mind struggled to remember where I was.

After some thought, I remembered passing some nearby cottages that I had seen signs for during my drive just a few moments ago, so I decided to take him there. There were no hospitals or police stations nearby where I could have gotten help, but I had been trained in trauma a few years ago and could provide the basic treatment he needed immediately if he was to survive.

It was a challenge to get him into my car though. He was completely unconscious, and he was well over 90 kilos. The rain had managed to completely soak the both of us, which made it more difficult for me to hold on to him. I drove my car as close as I could to the edge of the road and slowly managed to pull him into the back seat. The song, "Zindagi Pyaar Ka Geet Hai", was still playing on the radio as I rested the man in the car.

With the light from inside the car, there was a slightly better view of his body. Most of his cuts were not as deep as I had initially thought, but he did have a stab wound that deeply cut into his back. He was losing blood fast. I could see it spilling over my hands. I needed to apply pressure to his wounds to slow down his blood loss, but there was just too much for me to handle at a time. I had a suitcase full of clothes in the trunk, so I quickly grabbed an arm-full of clothing and began to tie them tightly around his wounds to apply enough pressure. I laid him on his side, but because he was over six feet tall, his legs hung off the back seat.

The rain was still heavy, and to make sure that he didn't face any additional injuries, I had to drive somewhat slowly to the local cottages. If my car was to skid because of the wet roads, there would be no chance for his survival. But I was losing time.

After what seemed like hours but, in reality, was only a few minutes, I reached the entrance of the cottage property. Leaving him in the car momentarily, I ran into the main building to see if I could have someone help me take care of the man's injuries.

At the desk, there was a man similar to the age of the injured man, but perhaps a few years older. He too was quite built and had a full beard, but unclean and thicker than that of the man in my car. His overall stature also seemed more aggressive and less neat. He was wearing a stained black t-shirt with some holes dispersed throughout it, and his jeans were covered in paint drips. He was cleaning the desk and was pressing the water out of a dirty wash cloth as I stepped inside.

When he saw me, his eyes widened, and he stepped back in shock for a moment, almost in fear. I then realized that he was lost at the fact that I was covered in blood. I didn't even notice until that moment, but the man's blood had become drenched in my own clothing along with the rain.

I quickly told him what had happened and that I was looking for a place to stay. I decided not to ask for help like I had originally planned because of the drunken state the cottage owner seemed to be in. His eyes were bloodshot from what may have been a long night, but he had a stench of alcohol that cut through the air. He looked so tired, yet he had this cruel look across his face. I even began to question whether I had made the right decision in coming here, but my options were limited.

The man told me that there was only one cottage available and it was the most expensive cottage of them all - a honeymoon cottage. I knew immediately that he was trying to con me out of my money - I had passed what looked like several empty cottages on the way to this building. He knew I was in an emergency and took it to his advantage. But I had no other option - no time to argue. This was the only place to stay for kilometers and the man resting in my car needed at least some care immediately. So I decided to take what the cottage owner said was available to me. I paid for the cottage, got the room key, and drove about a half kilometer to the vacant cottage, with a stranger strapped to the back seat.

The rain only seemed to be getting heavier. I parked my car as close as I could to the cottage, but there was still enough distance between my car and the cottage door to make it a challenge for me to get the man inside. There were also several steps in front of the cottage, and even before I could attempt to get the man inside, I knew I couldn't. His injuries could be fatal, and I would only have the capacity to pull him across the floor because of his size. Before I could find someone else to help, the owner from the reception desk called out to me in the rain.

"Do you need some help?" His tone of voice was sarcastic, and I didn't want his help, but I needed it. No one else was there to help me instead.

"By the way, I'm Arbazz." He held his hand out, expecting to shake mine. I ignored it. Something about him made me feel that something was off.

"If you could help me get him insi-"

"No problem," he said quickly as his eyes seemed to pierce into me. It made me feel so uncomfortable. And as much as I wanted him to leave, I needed him to help get the injured man inside.

Arbazz helped me carry the man by placing the man in between the both of us and placing the man's arms around each of our shoulders. Arbazz's hand slowly brushed across my shoulder and down my back. I could feel him slightly tugging at the back of my bra.

"Don't touch me. I don't need your help anymore," I said sternly as I stopped walking with Arbazz.

"It was an accident. Anyway, he's a heavy guy and you're a small girl," he said with a grin. "You need m-"

"I don't."

"Well, I'm going to help."

He moved his hand away from me and gripped on to the man's waist to lift him more easily. He turned on the light as we got inside and helped place the man on the bed.

Arbazz never lifted his eyes off me. The way he looked at me made me feel disgusted - like he was mentally undressing me from the way he stared. He seemed to purposefully be ignorant of the injured man covered in blood on the bed. I gestured to him that I no longer needed him anymore, and after an awkward hesitation from him, he slowly moved towards the door.

As he was walking to the door, he said, "Mandira's your name, right? I saw it on your ID when you checked in. Beautiful."

I pointed my hand in the direction of the door. My mind was more focused now on getting him outside of this room. He finally stepped outside but turned at the door to face me.

"It was nice meeting you Mandira. Congratulations on your honeymoon - oh, and if you need *anything more*, don't hesitate to ask. My cottage is just down the hill to the right if you are ever feeling the need for a visit." Again, his tone was harsh...vulgar, and he spoke with a crude grin on his face. I closed and locked the door on him as soon as I could.

I was able to see the injured man more clearly with the lights of the cottage. He was completely unconscious - his body as limp as a dead man. Patches of blood in different shades of red had appeared on his clothes with the passing time. The clothing I had tightly wrapped around his wounds were slowly becoming drenched in his blood, though his overall blood loss seemed to have slowed down.

I had an emergency kit in my car - it was something I always left in my car after working with victims of human trafficking. Having some experience treating people on roadsides, I learned that basic tools and simple procedures were sometimes enough to save a life. With that, I also learned that time was essential, and at the moment, it was slipping away from me.

After seeing that there was no sight of Arbazz, I quickly grabbed my emergency kit. There were clean sponges, medications, bandages, stitches, scissors, and everything else I may have needed to treat the man to a somewhat better condition.

I first took out the scissors and began to cautiously cut the man's clothes off. I had no idea how long he may have been on the side of the road, but his blood was still fresh on some parts of his body and dry at other parts. I needed to take off some of his clothes to prevent them from sticking to his

42

skin and open wounds in addition to being able to see exactly where he had been stabbed. I was left with his bare body on top of the bed sheets, with patches of blood and wounds that ranged in depth across his body.

He had three separate stab wounds on his chest and one long gash across his back in addition to the several bruises that covered his body. There was a cut across his cheek that I didn't notice before, but it wasn't deep and was a cut that would easily heal but that could surely leave a scar.

I took the sponge out of my kit and ran it under some cool water. As gently as possible, I cleaned his body to get rid of the excess blood. I had to take breaks to clean off the sponge because of how much blood there was. He also had a severe gash in the upper part of his chest. My one major concern now that his blood loss had slowed down was that his lungs would collapse because of air entering the open wound. He was breathing, and I needed to make sure that he continued to do so.

As I was putting in his stitches, I noticed a graceful look to his face - a sense of gentleness. He was the first sign of hope I had seen since the explosion, which was confusing for me at the same time, considering the seriousness of his condition. But in that moment, this was my mindset: I couldn't save a single person in that hospital, but I was going to save him.

Once I finished cleaning his body and stitching up his wounds, I pulled the bed covers from under him and exchanged them for a clean set that was folded in the closet. I gently pulled the sheets to his waist and went into the bathroom to take a shower.

It was the first time I had looked into the mirror since everything had happened. My eyes were tired, and my body was drenched in blood and rain. I washed my face with cool water as I watched the blood rinse into the drain. It reminded me of the blood orange of those flames - the loss of so much life. As I bathed, my mind was somewhere and, at the same time, was nowhere. I had no thoughts.

As I stepped out of the bathroom, I took a look at the clock. It was 4 a.m., so I decided I should get some rest, hoping that I wouldn't be kept awake by today's nightmare.

At the base of the bed, I saw that there was a black couch where I could sleep. Before I went to lie down, I checked on the man - his body was slowly stabilizing. His body was returning to a normal temperature and his heart rate was regulating, though it was faster than normal. Only time could tell me how his condition would improve. I then grabbed another clean sheet out of the closet, turned off the lights, and exhausted, closed my eyes as I rested my head on the soft arm of the couch.

***

I woke up around 7 a.m. as the sun was still rising. Even though I had slept around just three hours, I felt better refreshed than I was the day before. The man was still asleep. His face looked calm, and he seemed better stabilized. As I replaced some of his bandages, I noticed how his heart rate and breathing were slowly improving. He was healing...a miracle I would say.

I could hear a rooster's call in the distance as the sun's rays were beginning to shine slowly through the windows. I needed some fresh air, so I decided to walk around and check out the cottage and its surroundings.

The cottage itself was a simple, yet cozy one. It had clean white paint with wooden doors and an orange tile roof. Inside the cottage, there was a small bathroom, a king-sized bed, a bedside table, a desk with a table lamp, the black couch that I had slept on, and a fireplace. At the backside, there were five steps which led to two massive glass doors that opened to a patio with a small, but elegant dinner table and semi-balcony that looked out onto a small lake. The immediate surroundings of the cottage consisted of so much greenery, and in the distance, the small glow from a window of another cottage was just barely visible.

The honeymoon cottage was the most elevated of the cottages as it rested on the gradual slope of a hill, almost as if the cottage foundation consisted of a stepped platform. It was

also the farthest away from any of the other cottages. Its

setting was one that fit the setting of my drive through the area:

isolation. But in that isolation, there was beauty. The sound of

the rain patting against the trees, the sound of crickets growing

and fading with the sunrise, and the sound of nature

encompassing everything and anything. It was beautiful.

Chapter 2

It was late in the afternoon when my stomach began to growl. I hadn't eaten in two days, but I guess everything that was on my mind was just keeping my appetite down.

I remembered that there was a small dining area near the reception desk, but I didn't want to have to face Arbazz again. At the same time though, I knew I needed to eat something - so I took my chances. If he was there, I would just leave.

Coming into the main building, there was no sight of Arbazz. In a way, the room's mood seemed to have changed from when I had first come in there last night. It was much brighter with the sunlight hitting every piece of furniture in the room as a result of the massive glass windows that covered the place. The dining area had four small tables that were neatly set with white table cloths and simple dining ware.

Yesterday's stench of alcohol was replaced with the

smell of fresh kadala masala. The scent of the spices made my stomach roar.

At the opposite end of the dining area, there was a young boy, perhaps fifteen or sixteen years old. He was wearing a simple white shirt and black dress pants and was standing over a bar table, eating some poori. I felt a little bad for him - it seemed so lonely for him to be working in such a deserted place like this.

"Hello," I said softly trying to not startle him. "I was wondering if I could grab something to eat."

His face lit up as he noticed that I was standing there. Like he was excited and surprised to see another person here.

"Hi Madam. Absolutely - have a seat and I shall get you a menu."

"Don't worry - I'll have what you're having - it looks really good and smells incredible."

"Oh, thank you, thank you Madam," he said as he picked up a clean plate. "It's homemade - my very own recipe. Poori and kadala masala."

He quickly got a poori and hot kadala masala for me and set it on my table with a smile. I think he could sense my eagerness to eat because he chuckled as he placed the plate in front of me. My stomach was also very audible to the both of us.

Breaking off the first piece of hot poori and dipping it into the masala, I could feel my hunger. It was delicious. I was very hungry, so of course, food always tastes better when you're hungry, but this dish was special. It reminded me of my days with Zindagi. Jamal and I loved poori and kadala masala - it was the iconic pair for us, aside from Kajol and Shahrukh Khan in *Dilwale Dulhania Le Jayenge* of course.

"Amazing...this food is so good," I said as I broke off another piece of poori.

"Thank you Madam - that means a lot," he said with an innocent smile.

"And I absolutely mean it - this food is amazing! And you don't have to call me Madam," I smiled. "What's your name?"

"Madhu."

"Nice to meet you Madhu - I'm Mandira. Have a seat," I said as I tapped my hand on the table in front of the empty chair. "Let's eat together."

He sat down with an expression of growing ease. His mannerisms reminded me of home.

"How long have you been working here?"

"I've been working here for the last two years. Sometimes, it can get a bit boring, but I've been able to develop my cooking with some of the free time I have," said Madhu with a positive attitude.

"The food is great. It really is," I said as I put some more curry on my plate. "Are you from this area Madhu?"

"No, I'm actually from Tamil Nadu. How about you?"

"I'm from Kerala."

In response, Madhu smiled and asked, "How are you?" in Malayalam. I smiled back listening to his Malayalam. He was adorable.

"I've learned it from some of the guests that have come through here," he laughed. "But my boss is very strict about using English - he thinks it's the only way we can get tourists to stay here."

"I think it's important to have that diversity of language," I said in Tamil. Madhu smiled and leaned forward, crossing his arms and resting them on the table.

"It's nice to hear you speak Tamil - no one ever speaks that around here. You have a slight accent when you speak it - but it's not a Kerala accent. More like a Northern accent."

I nodded at his observation as I swallowed some of my food. "I was adopted by a school teacher from Kerala. She made sure I learned Malayalam but talked to me in Tamil on many occasions because she believed that it was important for me to know the language of our sister state. The northern accent comes from my roots in Uttar Pradesh, but Kerala and Mumbai have become my new homes," I said as I tried to listen to my own accent to see how different it sounded from his. "What brought you here?"

"I'm trying to make some money to help support myself and my sister. My parents were abusive towards her...they wanted another boy, not a girl. And I couldn't take how they were treating her. So for the last five years, we've been on our own."

"Just you two?" I asked in awe.

"Yes."

"What's her name?"

"Meera," he said with a smile. "She just turned fourteen a few days ago. I didn't have enough money at the time, but on my way home today, I've saved up enough money to buy her some of our favorite treat - jalebi."

"You're a sweet boy Madhu. You remind me of my older brother Jamal. Him and his wife have loved jalebi ever since they were kids," I told him. "I'd love to meet your sister."

"I hope you get the chance to...she's here at the cottages every once in a while but most of the time, she's studying and preparing for her exams at her school," he said as he lovingly mimicked her opening a book. "My boss told me that you are here with your husband - can I get him anything?"

"Oh...he's not my husband," I said quickly. "I found him unconscious and beaten on the roadside last night, but because of the storm and some flooding, I couldn't get him to a hospital, so he's been resting here," I said as Madhu nodded in understanding. "But if you have any clothes that I can borrow for him to use, that would be great. I only have my clothes and I don't know how comfortable he would be if I put him in a dress." We both laughed at my poor joke.

"Absolutely Madam - I'll bring them to your cottage by this afternoon."

"Thank you Madhu."

We continued talking and eating...such a sweet kid. I felt like I was talking to my brother. And his story about him and his sister reminded me of my own life before Zindagi.

After we finished eating, I helped him clean up the dishes. It was just me and him and I wanted to get to know about him and his sister a little more.

55

"You mentioned how your sister spends a lot of time studying...does she know what she wants to go into when she's older?"

Madhu smiled as he was drying our plates with a white towel.

"A doctor. That's her dream," he said. "We both grew up quite poor. And we've never been to a doctor before. So at first I was wondering why she had chosen that path. But then I realized that there was no need for me to wonder. Both of us grew up really fast...never had the opportunity to spend time with friends, play outside...you know...the typical childhood stuff. Our parents were really abusive, so we grew up defending each other all the time."

For a moment, he paused and stared at the ground as a sorrowed expression came across his face. "One day, my father had taken off his belt and had used it to whip my sister's back until she couldn't stand anymore. The reason...I had attempted to teach Meera how to read one of my Spiderman comic books." He paused again, reflecting on their past. "After that, I remember both of us running away from home that very night. But no one noticed us. No one seemed to care. It was good that our own parents could not track us down, but when we got to the hospital, the only doctor there refused to help bandage my sister because we didn't have any money. Many people just stared as my sister was collapsed at my feet from the pain," he said as he pointed towards his feet in disappointment. "She wants to make sure that no one ever feels the way she did that night. And I will stand by her and make sure she reaches that dream of hers. That's what's brought me to this job. And as much as this job and my boss might make me feel like I'm worthless, I know that what I'm doing is helping my sister know that she is worthy. And that means the world to me."

My heart melted as he spoke with so much maturity and sincerity.

"You're incredible Madhu. I hope you know that. And if there's anything I can do to help you two, let me know. Both of you are so incredibly brave."

I was in awe of his strength and love for Meera.

"Thank you Madam. And thank you for helping me clean up," he said as he put the last dish away.

"No problem - and thank you for the delicious meal. And you don't need to call me 'Madam' Madhu."

As I handed him money for the meal and some extra for him and his sister, he gently pushed my hand back.

"No need for that Mada-, Didi," he smiled as he corrected himself. "Use that money for medicine to help that man."

"Don't worry," I said as I put the money in his hand. "I have enough to treat him. This is for you and your sister."

He humbly accepted.

As I was heading out back to the cottage, Madhu called out to me, "Didi!" I turned towards him. "My boss...he's aggressive and rude - it's a major reason as to why there's hardly anyone ever here. Be careful around him Didi - he's a man that has no consideration for others, especially when he's under alcohol."

I nodded as I took a mental note of his reminder. "Thank you again Madhu."

When I returned to the cottage, I picked my phone up only to realize that I forgot to turn my ringer on. I had three missed calls from Jamal and four missed calls from Sim. I called their home phone, and just before the first ring was about to end, Simran picked up the phone. I could hear Jamal in the background asking Sim if it was me. As they answered the phone with worry, I told them that there was nothing to worry about.

Before I had left the remains of the hospital, which was quickly surrounded by many police officers and news reporters, I had told Jamal that I just needed to go somewhere and that I would come back in the next few days. He told me to come home with him, but I just needed to be away from home momentarily...just to think I told him.

"Mandira - where are you? Are you okay? We just want to make sure that you're okay? I should have done someth-"

"Don't worry Jamal - I just need some time," I said as I took a breath. "I didn't get the chance to say thank you though - thank you for holding me back. I wasn't thinking and if I had continued to chase after that boy..."

"No, no Mandira - you were going to do what makes you who you are - risking your life to save even a single stranger. I'm so sorry Mandira - everyone at the station is trying to wrap their heads around what happened. If you need anything, please let us know."

"We're always here for you if you need us - we know the storm was crazy last night and wanted to make sure you were safe," said Sim.

"Thank you guys. I'm sorry I didn't pick up - I forgot to take my phone off the silent mode. Is there any more information as to what happened?"

"As of now, they believe there was more than one terrorist involved," said Jamal. "You and I are the only witnesses for the bomber that we saw, but the department believes there was someone else involved because of how intricately carried out the attack was and due to the planted

bombs in the rest of the hospital. We found that there were

nine bombs already placed throughout the floors before that

bomber came in. There are 132 bodies that have been

accounted for so far."

"Is there any information on the bomber we saw?" I

asked earnestly. "I felt like his face was telling me that he

didn't want to have that suit on."

"My officers are looking into him and investigating his

flat right now," said Jamal.

"I just can't believe it. It happened so quickly," I said

with shock and frustration in my voice.

"I know. I feel like so many of us are just in shock,"

added Jamal.

"Let me know if any more information comes out."

"For sure," said Jamal as he seemed to lose his breath

for a second. I could hear my nephew jumping onto his lap.

"Oh, hey Mandira, Rehan wants to say hello."

"Put him on the phone," I smiled.

"Hey Ammai!" said Rehan loudly into the phone.

"Hey Rehan Kutta - how are you?"

"I'm doing great Ammai - how about you?"

"I'm doing great too Kutta. How was your day?"

"Super awesome Ammai!" responded Rehan with excitement. I could hear him fiddling with a wrapper in his hands. "The teacher was giving out candy to all the students today because it was her birthday - delicious chocolates," he said joyfully. "I snuck one extra for you too," he whispered.

When I first met Rehan, I took him to a chocolate factory run by a friend of mine. Ever since then, we've shared a special bond over chocolate, especially since Jamal and Sim hate that stuff.

"Aww thank you Rehan. When we get together soon, I'll bring a full bag of chocolates and you and me can hang out, eating all the chocolates we want and watching *Scooby Doo*. Cool?"

"Cool!" responded Rehan immediately. "I miss you Ammai."

"I miss you too Kutta."

"Love you Ammai. Umma," he said in his cute little voice.

"Umma. Love you Rehan."

Rehan then gave the phone back to Sim and Jamal. I love that kid with all my heart. He always manages to get me to escape the pain of reality, even if it's just for a few seconds.

I gave them the address to the cottage I was staying at, just in case of any emergencies, but I assured them that I just needed some time. I didn't tell them about the man that was sleeping just a couple of feet from me though. I didn't want them to be more worried than they already were. Hearing that a stranger was sleeping in the same cottage that I stayed in would pull that trigger for them.

"I love you guys."

"We love you too Mandira - stay safe," said Sim.

"I will. I'll talk to you guys soon."

After putting down the phone, I just roamed around the cottage area. The fog and mist added a sense of coziness to the surroundings, and with the cool breeze and nature that surrounded me, I finally began to come to terms with my emotions. I stood, with complete silence aside from the chirps of some birds, staring beyond a hill that overlooked an immense landscape of lush greenery and the sounds of a flowing river.

It was at that moment that I began to take in everything that had happened in the last two days. It was the first time I actually thought deeply about everything that had occurred instead of just trying to push it outside of my mind. All this time, I had continually thought of all the possible things I could have done to change what had happened...all of the things that could have saved the lives of those 132 people. But in the moment that I just looked at my surroundings...so beautiful and so serene, my heart finally accepted that Nima was gone. It accepted that there was nothing I could have done to prevent what had happened. But I promised her justice and that was something I would not let go.

As I looked out to the setting sun, a tear fell down my cheek, not as a result of pain, but as a result of the peace of mind that I had reached suddenly and so randomly in that moment. Sometimes, it's the journey to peace that can be so painful and difficult to get through. It would still take time for my mind and memory to heal, but I was getting there.

***

When walking back inside, I checked on the man to see if there were any changes in his condition. He was still in a deep sleep, with his face holding a dream-like expression.

His wounds were on their way to healing. I applied a little more medicine to his cuts to aid in the healing process and to prevent any source of infection as well.

As I gently rubbed the medicine against his wounds, I noticed how muscular the man was - his frame was quite built, and to the touch, I could feel his strength. It was a strength that I thought would be invincible against any attack. It made me wonder how he had gotten into the condition that he was in.

As I was washing my hands to get rid of the extra residue from the medicine, the electricity went out. It was 9:17 p.m., so I decided to get some rest.

***

Suddenly, at around 3:30 a.m., I woke up to the sound of aggressive and terrified mumbling. I got up from my couch to see that the man was still in bed, but he seemed to be having some kind of nightmare. I turned on the bedside lamp to find him with his forehead covered in sweat and his entire body heating up. I pulled down his sheets to just below his torso and increased the air conditioning to cool his body down. I grabbed the jug of water from the bedside table, poured a small amount of the cold water into my hand, and gently washed his face to help cool him down. With his eyes still closed, he relaxed a bit more and gradually went back to a deep sleep. I gently moved the hair that rested upon his forehead and felt the warmth of his skin.

This man was a mystery to me. Who he was, where he had come from, how he had gotten into the condition that he was in... these were questions that surrounded my thoughts. But there was something about him...something special that I couldn't figure out.

***

It had been two days since I had stayed in this cottage. The man was the most stabilized he had been, and I needed to get back home soon because I was a witness in the terrorist attack and needed to prepare for further investigations. The roads were still harsh to get through, but I wasn't needed here anymore - I was needed back home.

I stopped by the main building one last time. I had wanted to leave my number with Madhu just in case there was an emergency. The man was not in need of immediate medical attention anymore and it would be best to transport him to a hospital once the roads were more clear. He would be worse off stuck on a road for several hours than to be well rested here at the cottages. As I signed the paperwork needed to reserve the room for the man for a few more days, Madhu prepared a cup of hot porridge and gave it to me before I left so that I could eat something before the long drive back.

"Are you sure he doesn't need medical attention?" asked Madhu as I returned his pen.

"He needs it, just not right away," I said. "The storm is on and off right now and it's too much of a risk to take him on such a long drive to the closest hospital, especially if some of the roads haven't cleared yet."

"Does he need any medicine?"

"Yes, I've left a sheet of directions on how to treat him and my phone number in case. I have a few more creams that can be put on his wounds - just make sure to wash your hands before you apply the medicine to prevent him from getting infected. When he wakes up, he can be transported to a hospital."

"Do you think he will wake up?" he asked as I was putting the dabba he gave me into my bag.

"I know he will," I said in return. I trusted that the man would be alright. I could feel that time was on his side after seeing how quickly he seemed to be healing.

"You like him, don't you?" asked Madhu with a smile.

"I don't even know him," I said, trying to ignore the strange truth in his observation.

"Yeah, but you like him," he laughed as he waved his finger. "If you could have stayed longer, I think I could have watched a love story happen right in front of me," he said as he outlined the air in front of him with his hands. "Maybe he'll wake up with no memory of his past, and you'll be the love of his life who was destined to save him," he added as he pointed towards me.

"I feel like this story you're hoping for has to do with you watching *Mr. Bechara* last night," I laughed.

"I'm from the land of Sridevi - can you blame me?" he chuckled.

"I guess not," I laughed. "I'll send help for him once I get back to the city. I wish you and your sister the best. The hope you have for each other is phenomenal - don't ever let go of that Madhu."

"We'll hope to never let that go," he said with a smile. "Keep in touch Didi."

"Absolutely. If you two ever need anything, let me know. Know that I will always be someone that will be there for you two."

***

After coming back to the cottage, I set my bag on the small table in the room and began packing some of my clothes into my suitcase when my phone began to ring with its DDLJ ringtone. Before I could answer the call, the tone ended, and I couldn't retrieve enough connection to call back whoever it had been.

"Is that the tune of DDLJ?" said a deep and slightly groggy voice.

"Yea-"

I turned to face him as soon as I realized it.

He was awake.

Chapter 3

For a few moments, we stared at each other in silence, and personally, in shock. I believed that he would wake up, but I didn't expect it to be so quickly.

"Thank you for saving my life - I know I wouldn't have made it past that day if you hadn't helped me," said the man.

For a few more moments, I stared in silence and in shock.

"What's your name?" he asked, breaking the silence.

"Mandira," I responded, leaving my mouth open afterwards. I stared in shock again.

"Beautiful name," he said as he looked into my eyes warmly.

"What's your name?" I asked in return.

"Kabir," he smiled.

"Do you remember what happened to you?"

"The last thing I remember was hitting the pavement of a road," he said as he reached to feel the back of his head. "Some men were chasing me, but I don't remember why. They grabbed my wallet and then just beat me at that roadside I guess until I lost consciousness."

Without even realizing it, I had come closer to the bed to get a better look at him...to convince myself that he was really awake.

"Mand- ah!" he moaned in pain as he held his hand over the deepest wound on his chest.

I quickly put my hand on his wound as well. His hand was on top of mine...it was as if I knew his pain just as much as he did. There was a moment of silence between the two of us once again - our eyes met momentarily, but I looked back down at his chest while he kept looking at me.

"Just relax Kabir." Kabir...it was the first time I had said his name.

Slowly, I could feel some tension in his chest ease a bit.

"I need to get you to a hospital to get you checked out for any other possible internal injuries - I haven't been able to do so though because the roads haven't completely cleared up."

"What happened?" he asked with confusion.

"There was a huge storm - none of that comes to memory?"

"No... it's strange...I can't remember anything," he said as he seemed to be trying to recollect any hint of what had happened to him.

"Well it seems like your head had been hit pretty hard...I wasn't even sure if you'd wake up when I first saw you."

"I can live without the memory for now then," he said with a laugh, making me smile.

"Can I get you something to eat...you've been here for two days without anything."

"I'm good for now, thank you though," he responded graciously.

"Yeah, no problem. Just let me know if you need anything."

"Is there any way I can repay you for everything you've done for me?" he asked, gesturing towards the stitches I had done across his chest.

"Don't worry about it. I'm just glad you're getting better now."

"Looks like you're getting ready to leave," he said as he nodded his head in the direction of my suitcase.

"Oh...yeah...I have some things to take care of back home."

"Where's home?"

"About a six-hour drive from here - central Mumbai. Do you remember if you live around here?"

"I'm from central Mumbai too!"

"Any idea of what brought you all the way here?"

"I ... I don't remember," he said with a confused look on his face again.

"If you're feeling stable enough, I can drive you to the closest hospital. It's a bit of a long drive from here," I said as I looked down at my watch. "But the faster you get checked, the better off you'll be."

"That would be great. I'll just get a little washed up, and I'll join you back."

"Sounds good."

Slowly, with visible pain in his steps, he got out of bed. I could hear the taps of his heels as he walked across the room's wooden floor. I was surprised he could walk at all - the size of the cuts in his legs were enough to keep him paralyzed with pain.

As he stepped into the bathroom, I continued to pack my things. He seemed like a nice guy...a good man.

After about fifteen minutes, Kabir stepped out of the bathroom with a towel wrapped around his waist. His body seemed to radiate strength - the lines of his abs outlined by the water that streamed down his chest. I couldn't stop myself from looking at him, but I caught myself to make sure I didn't look like I was staring.

"Umm...I'm sorry Mandira..." he said as he held his towel with one hand and put his other hand on his head, running his fingers through his wet hair. "Are there any clothes that I can wear?"

"Yeah..." I said as I scanned the room to see where I had placed some clothes. "Yeah, here they are," I said, pointing towards the black couch right in front of me. I picked up the clothing set Madhu had given me for Kabir - a white dress shirt and black pants. When he walked back into the bathroom, I couldn't help but smile. Kabir was very handsome.

***

While I was packing, Kabir came over to help me. He looked really nice in the white shirt and black pants, and his hair was still wet from his shower. There was a simplicity to him that was warm.

"So what brought you all the way here?" he asked.

"I just needed to get my mind off some things going on back home - thank you for helping me do that. That first night I saw you...I don't think I've ever seen so much blood in front of me. Definitely got my mind off some things."

"My pleasure," he said with a laugh.

I smiled as I continued packing.

Today was particularly nice weather. There was a cool breeze and not much humidity at all. The sky was cloudy...I could tell that more rain was coming. The air was thin with the higher elevation of the land - I could feel each and every breath of mine.

Kabir slowly helped me get my bags into my car. His bandages were now off, and I could see his dried wounds glisten under the sun. As I got into the car, I continued to look at Kabir - he was so genuine, so caring, even in the few moments I had actually spoken with him. There was a feeling in my heart I had never felt before when I looked at him, as Bollywood as that may sound. I, in a way, didn't want to leave anymore. I wanted to stay...I wanted to get to know him more...to understand him more. And, in the next few moments, it seemed that God was listening to my heart this time.

When I put the key in, the engine hiccupped and shut off. I tried again, but this time, there was not one sound from the ignition, but there was a slight burning smell. I got out of the car, pulled up the hood, and saw that the motor was burnt out. There was no way of getting it to start at that point. And in such a distant and isolated location, there were no buses or taxis. Kabir came to the hood of the car and checked the engine as well. Before I said anything, he looked up at me with a gentle smile on his face.

"Can I help you take your bags back inside?"

"That would be great, thanks," I said with a sigh.

And with that, the monsoon rains began to pour heavily, mixing with the stormy winds. As I stood, bent over the hood of the car, I looked towards the side and faced the cloudy sky, wondering what kind of game God was trying to play.

***

As dinner time approached, both of our stomachs began to grow with hunger. There wasn't much to eat, and the reception dining area was closed for tonight. I did have a couple of bars of kadalai mittai though, so Kabir and I decided to split that for dinner.

"Have you lived in Mumbai all your life?" I asked, cutting the mittai.

"My family is actually originally from Pakistan, but I was born and raised in Punjab. Both of my parents are farmers and they enjoy the simple lifestyle that Punjab allows for - away from city lights and all," he said as he motioned towards the ceiling to represent the city lights.

"That must be really nice. I've heard Punjab is so beautiful - it's one of my dream places to visit."

"Because of the Punjab setting in DDLJ?" he humorously responded, grabbing a piece of mittai.

"You're really getting to know me a lot faster than I thought you would," I laughed. "So, what brought you down to Mumbai?"

"I work as a travelling teacher. I spend a few months in a different place and help set up foundations for education where there is none. Punjab, Kashmir, Goa...you name it, I've been there."

"That sounds amazing. What's been your favorite place so far?"

"Punjab for sure...that's home for me."

"Do you go back often?"

"I try to, but my first priority is always the kids - I go where they are," he said as he smiled.

"I think teachers deserve the world. I feel like they do so much...but sometimes it seems like the world doesn't see it or rather chooses to ignore it," I said, reflecting on how so many of my teachers were treated.

"It's unfortunate that in so many places, teachers aren't respected. But I've lived with the belief that it doesn't matter how certain people see a teacher. It's the kids and their perspective that matters for me...and I've learned that over time," he said. "Whenever I see a young kid write out their name for the first time, with so much excitement in their eyes," he said while mirroring a child writing, "or whenever I see one of my older students getting into university, it's meaningful to know that I had some role in helping them reach their dreams."

"Your words remind me of those of my grandmother."

"She must speak from experience as well."

"Yeah," I smiled as I remembered how excited she was when I was accepted into the police academy. "She was also a teacher."

"What did she teach?"

"Mathematics."

"My worst subject," he laughed.

"Mine too," I grinned.

"Great kadalai mittai by the way - it's been a while since I've had this," said Kabir as he looked at the piece in his hand.

"Thank you - it's actually homemade…Zindagi's recipe."

"Zindagi?"

"That's my grandmother."

"Cool name for a grandmother."

I smiled, forgetting that most people didn't refer to their grandmothers with that name.

"How about you?" asked Kabir. "A Mumbai girl all your life?"

"It's a bit complicated," I said as I wiped my hands with a small towel. "I was born and raised in Uttar Pradesh for nine years, but I was then raised by my grandmother. She's not my grandmother by blood but most people referred to her as grandmother in our town, so that's how I learned to refer to her. Seeing the condition my family was putting me in, she took me to Kerala with her to protect me and give me a better future than I could have ever imagined."

"What happened...if you don't mind me asking. Do you still have family in Uttar Pradesh?"

"Yeah, no worries. I do...I believe my parents and two older brothers are still there...I just haven't seen them in fourteen years. When I was growing up, so many people, including my own family, would put in the effort to make it known to me how undervalued a girl is in society. They pulled me out of my education to fund the best education for my brothers and would threaten to sell me into prostitution whenever I tried to read their books. When I was nine years old, my parents introduced me to an older man, perhaps in his thirties. I distinctly remember him having this ragged scar under his left eye. We all sat in the living room, drinking tea and eating banana chips, but at such a young age, I didn't even realize what they were doing to me. It was my older brother who came and explained what was going on. He told me that they were going to marry me off to that older man...at nine years old."

"How could they..." he asked with shock.

"It was a financial opportunity for them. I was a burden in their eyes. And at the time, I didn't realize how common the practice was," I shrugged regretfully, shaking my head.

"That evening, once everyone had slept, I remember my brother, Varun, coming to me and telling me to run away from that house. He was always the brother that I could trust...he would always end up stealing some money from my father so that he could buy me some books to read. He helped me pack my bags and told me that everything would be fine as long as I found a home somewhere else. I remember both of us walking out onto the road when the lights in my house suddenly turned on. My parents were awake, and Varun could not come with me."

Kabir shook his head in disbelief.

"I can remember him earnestly saying, 'Run as far as the moon's light can guide you and believe that goodness always exists in the world, especially during the tough times.' Those were his last words to me," I told Kabir.

"I ran away. I ran away as far as I could from that house with nothing but the clothes that I had on and one hundred rupees that my brother had stolen from my father's wallet. I forgot the bags we had packed in the urgency to leave.

I remember how heavy it was raining that night...I knew I needed shelter and being so hungry that evening...I ended up stopping at a small tea shop, where I ran into a woman. Her name was Kavita D'Souza."

"Zindagi?"

"Yes, that's her," I said with a smile. "She saw me all alone in the middle of the night trying to get something to eat. She ended up paying for my meal...I still remember...fresh poori and kadala masala. It was the first time in my life that I had gotten to eat a whole plate of food for myself. And she sat with me, talking to me as if I had value...a sense of value I had never felt before." I smiled to myself as I thought of our coincidental meeting.

"At first, I thought she was treating me nicely to get something in return. It's something that happens a lot with kids on the streets too...they have no place to go and suddenly, strangers treat them with respect momentarily only to pull them into begging or sex trafficking. I thought I'd eat quickly and run off after, but as she talked to me, I realized she wasn't a stranger...not that kind of stranger."

"When did you start calling her Zindagi?"

"As soon as I moved to Kerala to stay with her. She started to tear up as I told her my story that night at the tea shop...it was at that moment that I knew I could trust her...never had anyone attempted to understand my feelings until that point in time. And I could see that true sense of love in her eyes...that true compassion she held in her heart. She decided that she wanted to take care of me...protect me. The next day, she purchased two train tickets and took me to Kerala with her."

"You really did put your faith into her."

"When I think of the story from a general perspective, it sounds so risky. A nine-year-old girl heading to a completely different state on the opposite end of India with a stranger. But it was the best risk I've ever taken. It's what made me who I am today. She was the first person to show me the true meaning of life...taught me what it meant to live life on my own terms. I can't imagine what would have happened to me had I stayed just a few more hours with my family in Uttar Pradesh. I still remember that older man's face to this day. But Zindagi gave me my first home. Kerala is a home for me."

"She sounds like an incredible woman."

"Definitely."

"So she's your family."

"Yes - her and my older brother, Jamal. Soon after I was adopted, Zindagi surprised me one day when she walked into our home with an eleven-year-old boy in a clean new outfit with nothing but a beautiful mandolin in his hands," I said as I outlined the shape of the mandolin. "He was actually the one to introduce me to DDLJ - that tune was always his favorite to play on the mandolin. He had grown up in the slums of Delhi and my grandmother had just met him while she was speaking with some of her nun friends at Church. She said she loved his charm and simplicity and saw that he needed a home because the orphanage could no longer house him when he turned twelve."

"Is he still living in Kerala?"

"He shifts between Kerala and Mumbai every six months. He mainly works as a teacher too."

"Hmm..." said Kabir.

"What?" I asked him.

"D'Souza, Jamal, Mandira...a Christian, a Muslim, and a Hindu all in a household...seems like something we need more of in the world."

"I always laugh thinking about it because it reminds me of one of those jokes... 'If a Christian, Muslim, and Hindu were to walk into a bar...' but the only thing that happened was the growth of our respect and love for each other. I couldn't agree with you more - we do need more mutual understandings about religion and its differences.

We really got the best of three worlds. Zindagi made sure to let us continue in the faith we believed in. She always respected our religious differences and even taught me some Hindu prayers while teaching Jamal some of his Islamic prayers. She would go to Church every morning, and whenever possible, Jamal and I would join her. The Church she went to was always so beautiful," I said, trying to illustrate its grandiosity with my hands. "I couldn't understand the Mass - the Malayalam spoken is somewhat different in style...but she would always answer any questions we had after Mass was over. I learned a lot...but I think I learned the most about being a good human being from her."

"So you learned about zindagi through Zindagi."

"Exactly," I laughed.

"I'd love to meet her one day."

"I wish you could too," I said as I looked to the floor. "Three years ago, she was killed in a suicide explosion near Ernakulam. In an instant...I lost her...it was as fast as the instant when she had changed my life fourteen years ago."

"I'm so sorry Mandira."

"No worries. She was more than a mother to me. It took me some time to accept that she was gone, but she's in a good place now. She was starting to get sick...she was seventy-four years old...she felt as if her time was coming to an end. Just a few days before she was killed, she sat down with me and Jamal to tell us that she'd always be watching over us...making sure that the world would not do us harm. She said to watch for God's special sign - the rain. It was with the rain that I had met her. It was with the rain that Jamal got in trouble and ended up coming to Church, eventually meeting our grandmother that one day many years ago. She always said, 'With the rain, there is a sign from God.'"

"Then I think God is really trying to tell you something Mandira...with all this rain," said Kabir as he pointed to the window.

"Yeah it seems like it," I laughed again.

"And Jamal?"

"I think you would love Jamal. He's in Mumbai right now with his wife, Simran, and their six-year-old son, Rehan - the absolute cutest little boy I've ever seen. Jamal works to mentor children who have faced abuse, especially for those who are now in orphanages. That's why he shifts between Mumbai and Kerala. He also heads to Delhi every once in a while, especially to look after the orphanage he set up in the slums where he grew up."

"Wait...what's the name of the orphanage?" asked Kabir eagerly.

"Zindagi's Home for Children."

"I've been there before...about nine months ago," he nodded. "Wait, does your brother have a sleeve tattoo?"

"Yeah that's him. Wow - that's amazing! A really small world I guess. You were there teaching?"

"Yes, and he was the one who introduced me to all the kids. But all of those kids called him Raj?" he said, squinting his eyes and trying to figure out if he remembered correctly.

I laughed at his confusion. "Remember how I said he was the one that introduced me to DDLJ? He loves that film more than anyone I've ever met. And his wife's name is Simran, so all the kids tell him that he's her Raj. That's where the name comes from."

"That's actually really cute," he said as he sat back and smiled, resting his forehead from squinting.

"It really is...all of those kids actually helped him propose to her too. They just got married about a year ago."

"Wow - that's very sweet! And Varun?"

"That night was the last time I ever spoke to him...I don't know where he is now...or even if he's alive after helping me escape. In fact, the last piece of news I heard from where I lived in Uttar Pradesh was that the man that I was supposed to marry married another girl...twelve years old. I heard she was beaten so badly, and in less than a year, she died during childbirth...twelve years old...I still carry the guilt of that. It could have been me in her place...she could have lived had I never run away."

"Mandira...you know you can't carry the guilt for what he did..."

"I know," I sighed, "but it's something that's been difficult for me to move forward with...I always think about how that girl may have felt...scared...alone...who she would have been today...all questions that only leave guilt as their answers," I said as I shook my head in frustration. "How about you? Any siblings?"

"I have an older brother - Shahir - and his wife, Alizeh, who we call Ali. She's like an older sister to me. They're both living in Punjab and both are working as physicians. Shahir is a cardiologist and Alizeh is an OB-GYN. They've both always been so passionate about the medical field and using that to make their impact," he said as he rested his hands on his knees. "How about you?"

"What do you mean?"

"What's your passion?" he clarified.

"The same as yours...teaching."

"Really! Looks like it's a family art," he smiled.

"Yeah," I smiled back. "My brother, Sim, and I work with young kids, mostly girls, who have been rescued from abusive homes and human trading. Jamal and Simran grew up in the slums too, so they really understand the conditions that many of those kids have lived in."

"You seem to have some medical knowledge under your belt as well based on what I see from my stitching," he said, gently brushing his hand against some of his stitches.

"I have some basic trauma training. It's something that became necessary once I started working with victims of abuse. One of the nuns from Church taught me everything I know when it comes to a medical emergency. The medical field was always something that fascinated me, and Sister Marina helped me foster that fascination."

"I'm really glad she did," he chuckled.

***

As we were sitting in the dimly lit cottage, with the rain loudly hitting the palm leaves outside, we, for a moment, looked into each other's eyes and simply smiled. It was a pure and simple moment of silence between the two of us...it was beautiful...she was so beautiful.

For the next few days, I began to know the Mandira that I wanted to get to know. She was sweet, genuine, intelligent, charming, funny...everything. And every moment I was with her, I always found myself smiling. She took away my pain...took away my internal sorrows, even though I couldn't even remember where the sadness was coming from. I had never felt this way about a woman before...God was sending me a sign this time.

Chapter 4

In the morning, we went fishing to find us some lunch. We had picked up the fishing lines from Madhu yesterday, found some worms for bait, and just decided to test our luck.

I don't think I've ever been so entertained before. Poor guy...after a while, Kabir caught a pretty good size fish, but the fish jumped out of his arms as soon as he tried to get a hold of it. He still kept such a positive and jokeful attitude - I loved it.

We ended up staying at the river until late afternoon that day. And after some more time, we both ended up catching two smaller fish. And he wasn't a bad cook either.

"Where did you learn to cook like this?" I asked as I took another bite of rice mixed with the fish.

"My grandfather," he smiled. "My favorite food has always been paneer butter masala, but as a kid, the only times I would get to eat it was when my mother made it, which was rare because most of my family didn't like the taste of paneer.

So one day, my grandfather showed me how to cook the dish on my own. I was surprised how I didn't end up getting tired of eating paneer. I can't tell you how many times I've made that dish since he's shown me how to," he said, shaking his head. "After that day I spent with him, I soon learned that I loved to cook. He taught me everything from tandoori chicken to gulab jamun - you name it, I can make it," he said confidently. "Over time, my grandfather and I developed a close relationship because of my passion to learn and his willingness to teach me."

"That's so sweet," I said in amazement. Kabir was funny, handsome, passionate about helping others, a good cook, and had a sweet family. Too good to be true I thought to myself. But that thought left my mind almost immediately. Kabir was genuine.

"He's definitely a sweet man," responded Kabir. "He's always the first one to welcome me home whenever I go back to Punjab. He's always sitting on the front porch with a towel hung over his shoulder and a newspaper in his hand. He runs a bakery back home and personally delivers food to every house in our village on a delivery bike."

"Oh, I think I've seen those kinds of bikes before...they're a bit like the mobile ice cream vendor bikes, right?"

"Exactly - the ones with a huge box attached to the backseat," he said, as he outlined the shape of the bike with his hands. "When I was a kid, I would join him on his rides around the village. I would sneak out a few of the snacks for myself every once in a while too. He makes the best cutlets and samosas. I've never been able to make them like he does," said Kabir as he stood up and grabbed both our glasses.

While Kabir was getting some more water for the both of us, we heard a knock at the door. Kabir opened it and standing outside was Madhu, peering into a brown bag.

"Hey Madhu. How have you been?" asked Kabir.

"Can't complain Bhai. Just had some extra food for you guys," he said, lifting his head away from the bag.

Immediately, Kabir and I noticed that he had a black eye.

"What happened to your eye?" asked Kabir with concern. "Are you okay?"

"Oh, nothing Bhai...boss was just a little drunk last night," he said, nodding it off like it was a usual occurrence.

"Arbazz did this to you?" I asked as I took a closer look at his eye.

"Don't worry Didi - I'll be okay. Thank you though."

"Madhu, has he done this before? Has he hurt you like this before?" I asked.

"A few times... he just got a bit upset because I burned a few roti," he said with some embarrassment.

"He shouldn't be treating you like this," I responded, putting a hand around his shoulder while still examining his eye. I put my other hand just over his eyelid and checked to see if there could be any possible internal damage. "We're planning on leaving in the next few days. Would you like to come with us? If he's willing to hurt you for something so simple, I don't want to leave you here."

"We'll be fine Didi. My boss gets upset sometimes, but this job pays well. I need the money for my sister."

"I can get you a paid job closer to the city and a place to live. It's up to you and your sister, but I can definitely help you two in any way that you may need," I emphasized.

"We don't want to become a burden for you," he said, shaking his head.

"You won't be a burden at all," responded Kabir. "I have an empty apartment in Mumbai that I rent out. You and your sister are absolutely welcome to stay there for free as long as you need."

"And I have a close friend of mine who works in the restaurant business," I added. "She's looking for some new cooks and I know that she will hire you in a heartbeat once she tastes one of your dishes."

A smile began to come across Madhu's face.

"If it's no problem, we would love to come," said Madhu.

"No problem at all Madhu," assured Kabir.

"Thank you so much. You have no idea how much this means to us!" he smiled. "My sister will be here tomorrow. I'll call her tonight and tell her about it. I know she'll be so excited. She's always wanted to live in the city of dreams. And you'll be able to meet her too. Thank you so much. Thank you," he repeated as he put his hands together in front of his chest and slightly bowed his head.

"Anytime for you Madhu," I said as Kabir patted Madhu's shoulder in comfort.

"Oh, I almost forgot!" exclaimed Madhu. "I've prepared some rice and lentil curry for you two. I have to go back into town to pick up some more roti and other food supplies for the restaurant, so I need to close the restaurant early tonight."

"It smells really good," I said.

"I second that," added Kabir. "Thanks Madhu."

Kabir carefully picked up the hot pot of curry and tiffin of rice from Madhu.

"You look like you're doing a lot better Bhai," said Madhu.

"Much better thanks to her," said Kabir as he nudged my shoulder with his. "I'm really lucky," he smiled.

As Kabir turned to rest the curry and rice on the table behind us, Madhu raised his eyebrows and gave me two thumbs up in response to Kabir's comment. I waved my hand at him, trying to tell him to let go of that love story idea.

"That's great to hear - I'm glad that you're doing well," said Madhu, quickly putting his hands down when Kabir turned to face him. "If you two need anything, here are the keys to the main building. Take whatever you need."

"Where is Arbazz?" I asked. "I haven't seen him since the first night here."

"He's most likely passed out drunk somewhere," shrugged Madhu. "I haven't seen him since last night when he hit me...but that's common for him."

I shook my head in disapproval.

"Thanks again for the food Madhu," I said.

"No problem. Have a good evening."

"You too. Stay safe," waved Kabir.

Kabir and I watched as Madhu got onto his bike and rode off into the darkness.

"Who's Arbazz?" asked Kabir as he shut the door.

"He's the owner of these cottages. He was completely drunk when I came here with you...and he took advantage of your condition and the need to get you treated as fast as possible. That's how we ended up in this honeymoon suite, despite the fact that the entire property is empty."

"That explains it...I was wondering if you had other intentions," he said with a laugh.

I rolled my eyes and laughed.

"Just a joke," he said as he smiled and held his hands up innocently. "Mandira, can I ask you a question?"

"Of course."

"You are a very positive and loving person - I can see that in the time we've spent together. But...why do I feel like I see sadness in your eyes?"

I smiled softly to the floor at his observation.

"I'm trying to stay positive, but I guess that's not really working. I've always felt like positivity can get rid of sadness. But it turns out that, sometimes, it only attempts to hide it," I said, shaking my head. "Remember how I told you that I came here to get my mind off some things."

Kabir nodded gently.

"There was an explosion at a hospital in Mumbai," I told him. "It happened the day that I found you. I was there when the attack happened - the entire building burst into flames after a suicide bomber came in. I can't help but think about it. I came all the way here, thinking I could somehow, for just even a moment, escape it...give myself some time to process it...but it just continues to consume my thoughts in different ways."

"You were there right before the explosion?" asked Kabir.

"I was just outside of the hospital doors when it happened. The fact that it happened is horrific...the fact that I knew so many of the people in that hospital is unbearable to me right now. I can see them in those flames...and I can't un-see that Kabir...I can't..."

Kabir gently put his hand on mine.

"I was never planning on coming back," I said, squinting my eyes trying to not cry.

My words became blurred. It was the first time I was saying this out loud. Kabir held my hand tighter and looked at me, his eyes a reflection of my sorrow.

"That night I found you on the roadside...I wasn't planning on trying to get back up again and live my life. I even packed a suitcase to make sure that Jamal didn't think I was so upset enough to...I was going to make it seem like an accident so that their pain wouldn't be so heavy."

I broke down into tears as Kabir held me close. "I'm sorry...I didn't mean to," I said, wiping away my tears.

"Don't be sorry - I'll always be here to listen," said Kabir as he hugged me gently and rested my head on his shoulder.

"I just felt the weight of all of the horrible experiences in my life suddenly. I've never been at such a low point in my life..." I couldn't help but cry. Thinking about the thoughts that I had that night was painful.

"No one deserves to hold on to this kind of pain," said Kabir as he stroked my hand. I took a deep breath as I was comforted in Kabir's embrace.

"I've come to terms with the idea that I couldn't do anything to change what happened...but my mind holds on to the pain of those who were killed that day. And to the pain of those who continue to be victims to some horrendous people. People that are protected by power and money and prestige. And I can't get myself to let go of it," I added. "But I've learned my lesson. If anyone ever tells you that I've killed myself, you'll know that it isn't true. I've promised myself to never act on those thoughts again. Looking back at that first night, you gave me a paddle of hope while I felt like I was drowning in a sea of hopelessness. I thought God was getting me to save your life, but, in a way, finding you that night saved mine. It gave me a paddle of hope…a needed one."

***

Just as we were about to finish dinner, Kabir suddenly got up and walked over to a radio that was sitting on the bedside table. He picked at the tuner momentarily and soon, "Yeh Raatein Yeh Mausum" was playing on the radio, echoing throughout our cottage, which was dimly lit by the corner fireplace.

"You mentioned that you love listening to these old Hindi songs," said Kabir with the dim light across his face and a gesture for my hand. I took him up on the offer, and to the tune of the old song, we danced. Our steps reflected each other's.

"You're not that bad on your feet," I said as I took note of his steps.

"I try...grandfather's advice...dancing and cooking...a good path to a woman's heart," he grinned.

"Your grandfather has taught you well. You're an impressive man Kabir."

"Well you're an impressive woman Mandira. I wouldn't even be on my feet had it not been for you. I've been trying to figure out exactly what about you makes you so special - there's just so much good about you."

"Your grandfather has really taught you well," I joked.

I looked into his eyes and he, into mine.

"What do you see?" he asked.

"A great cook. I see your handsome brown eyes. Someone who knows how to make me smile. What do you see?" I asked in return.

"Wonder Woman - you brought me back to life. I see your beautiful beautiful smile. Someone who makes me feel like everything is going to be okay."

***

The next day, we returned to the river, which branched off into a small lake. There, we found a few canoes and decided to take one for a ride. As we pushed the boat into the water and jumped in, we found a couple of paddles hidden under the seats and used those to move us further into the lake.

We had been at the cottages for almost a week now, and, in a way, I still didn't want to go back home. It was strange...he seemed perfect. In the last few days, I've laughed more than I ever have...Kabir just had this way of making me feel so comfortable. I've just been so happy despite my sorrow...even I can't explain it...it just felt right.

"I just love being on the water," said Kabir while running his hand through the water beside our boat. "There's something about it that's just so peaceful."

"Growing up in Kerala, boating has always been a big part of my life. Have you ever seen the snake boat races around Onam time?"

"No, but I've heard of them...vallam kali, right? They sound like a ton of fun."

"They are - I've seen them since I was ten and have been a part of them since I turned eighteen. Lots of good memories from those races."

"How did you get interested in them?" asked Kabir.

"Zindagi's older brother, Jai Papa, was a naval architect and owned a boating industry, and as kids, me and Jamal were always the first to get to join him on the test drives. But my favorites were always the most simple...the wooden canoes and the snake boats. Jai Papa would take me and Jamal to the races every year...we were always the loudest, rooting for the boat he had built. And in a few years, I ended up racing on the very same boats I used to root for."

"Want to race?" asked Kabir with excitement in his voice.

"What?" I asked to make sure I had heard him correctly.

"You versus me?"

113

"Are you sure?"

"Scared to lose?" he laughed.

"Oh, so that's how you want to play?" I said as I paddled swiftly through the water.

"I've poked the competitive side in you haven't I," he said as he paddled on the opposite side.

"Yes, you did...and let me tell you," I said as I leaned forward. "Competitive Mandira doesn't hold back."

"Neither does a competitive Kabir," he said as he lifted his paddle out of the water.

We paddled our canoe back to the shoreline. Kabir rolled up his sleeves and jumped out of the boat. Quickly, he ran to get another boat. In moments, he had pulled up another canoe and was getting ready to sit inside when he suddenly had this expression of child-like spontaneity come across his face.

"Let's make a deal," he said as he rested his arm on his bent knee. "If I win, I get to take you out on a date. We've been spending lots of time together, but I want to take you on a real and official date...you and me."

"Deal. And if I win, you'll cook up some of your delicious dishes for me. I look forward to a feast for a champion," I responded as I pounded my closed fist against the boat.

"I look forward to our date tomorrow night at 7 p.m.," he said with a wink and a wide grin.

We paddled our separate boats out into the middle of the lake and lined them up with a tree that was on the shore. From the way we had positioned ourselves in each of our boats, there was no doubt that we both held a competitive side.

"Whoever gets past that tree on the far right with the three coconuts at its base wins."

"Sounds good to me."

"Ready?" he asked.

"Ready," I said confidently as I kept my eyes forward.

"Ready, steady...go!" he yelled.

We were off...and kept at each other's pace. For someone who said he's never raced before, Kabir was quite fast. And for someone who was half dead about a week ago,

115

he was even faster. I was ahead of him, but just slightly. The water that was bouncing off his paddle was reaching my cheeks.

"My grandfather always said," shouted Kabir, "find your opponent's weakness and turn it into your advant-"

Suddenly, Kabir's voice broke off and I heard a much bigger splash. I turned for a second to see that his canoe had flipped over, but there was no sign of Kabir. I slowed down and kept looking out into the water for him...there was no sight of him. I didn't even know if he could swim. Was he drowning?

I jumped out of my boat and into the water. It was much deeper here...my feet couldn't reach the bottom and all I could see was darkness beneath me. There was no sight of Kabir.

I poked my head out of the water for a breath of air.

"Kabir! Kabir!" I yelled, but there was only silence in return.

Again, I went back underwater and tried to see any sign of him. Nothing.

Then, from the corner of my eye, I noticed my boat suddenly pacing forward. I swam above the water to see Kabir sitting in my boat, paddling his way to that tree on the far right.

"Kabir!" I shouted as I continued to keep myself afloat in the water.

"My grandfather always said...find your opponent's weakness and turn it into your advantage," he yelled in return across the water as he reached the finish line.

"Well played Mr. Malik...well played," I said out loud to myself.

I flipped Kabir's boat upwards and pulled myself up back inside. By the time I was paddling back to shore, Kabir was standing at the shoreline, with his arms crossed and smiling.

As my boat got closer, he ran into the water to help pull the canoe back on land.

"Tomorrow at 7."

117

"Your grandfather…I really need to meet him," I said with a smile. "You're damn good."

"You're damn too good," laughed Kabir. "That's why I had to use your goodness to my advantage," he chuckled.

"Goodness isn't a weakness Kabir," I said as I strained some of the water from my shirt.

"It's your weakness and your strength Mandira."

Chapter 5

I was falling in love with him...and in an unexplainable

way, I could feel his love for me. This wasn't just someone

looking for a girl to simply mess around with here and there.

There was more to his love... I could sense it from the warmth

of his character. I might have lost that race the other day, but a

date with Kabir wasn't such a bad outcome either.

Around 5 p.m., I decided to head into the main building

to give Jamal and Sim a call. I had called them a few days ago

to let them know that I wouldn't be home for a few more days.

Thankfully, they didn't ask any questions...they knew I still

needed some time away from home. And they still didn't know

about Kabir, and I wasn't going to tell them about him just yet

either. It would worry them...but there was nothing to worry

about. I'd be worried if I heard it in their shoes though.

The cellular connection was somewhat weak from the

cottage itself, but it was a bit better around the reception desk.

Enough to make a call. There was also a small computer in the dining area that I could use to check out recent news and my emails since the internet on my phone was so slow. Like I said, it had been a week since I had been home and with everything from the recent attack, there was bound to be a lot of news.

As I was heading into the dining area, Madhu came by and passed me a folded note.

"Didi - this is from Bhai. Looks like my *Mr. Bechara* prediction is really happening," he smiled.

"We'll see, we'll see," I responded laughing.

After handing me the note, he walked towards the door exiting the cottage restaurant with a glass of mango juice in his hand.

"How's your sister? Were you able to see her the other day?"

"I hope she's doing well. I got a phone call from her school saying that she needs to stay there a bit longer with the rest of the students since the storms have delayed their exams.

I haven't been able to talk to her though - when I asked to speak to her, they said that they took away the students' phones for exam security purposes after they found a student trying to share test answers. It worries me that we haven't been able to talk - I know how stressed she can get with exams like these sometimes. But I gave her my necklace and she gave me hers," he said as he pulled a necklace out with a pendant in the shape of the moon from under his shirt and showed me. "We're always with each other, even if we can't see or hear one another. I have her moon necklace - she's always been a night person. And she has mine, which has the sun - I have always been a morning person."

"A good balance between the two of you."

"Exactly," he laughed. "Goodnight Didi, I'll see you in the morning."

"Goodnight Madhu." I watched him disappear as he stepped out of the room.

The note itself was simple - a small square piece of white paper folded into a triangular shape. It read,

Yaad rakhna...meet me in the cottage balcony at 7 p.m.

– Kabir, Your Champion

I smiled as I refolded the note and placed it into my pocket.

Setting up the computer itself took some time...many of the wires were unplugged and some of the keys were falling off the keyboard.

While I was waiting for the internet connection to come through, I called Sim and Jamal's home phone. After three rings, Simran's voice came across. I could hear Rehan's favorite show, *Scooby Doo,* playing on the television in the background.

"Hello?"

"Hi Sim."

"Oh, hey Mandira - I'm so glad to hear your voice. How have you been? Everything's alright?"

"Yeah, I've been good...I'm doing good. Just wanted to check up on you guys."

"Mandira - they think they've identified the second terrorist."

"Really? Who?" I asked in a louder voice, eager to know who was responsible for the explosion.

"Ahmed Kazemi. Jamal says he looks really familiar... he thinks the man lives in our town."

"Is he older than the boy we saw?"

"Yes, mid-to-late twenties, I think. And he was the key planner for the attack. Jamal emailed you a picture this morning."

"I'm sitting at a computer right now, but the internet is taking some time to connect. I haven't been able to get access all week. Is there any other information on him?"

"Nothing else so far. There's an ongoing search for him though."

"Wait, he's alive?" I asked in surprise.

"The police believe he is. They have sources saying that he was seen after the explosion near the building Nima was found in. No one knows where he is though. There's a notice out for his arrest...I think Jamal has all the information in the email. Jamal said they were soon going to be dispatching all undercover agents to search for him...be careful Mandira...he's supposed to be heavily armed."

"I will. Send my love to Rehan and Jamal."

"For sure. Call me if you need anything - anything at all okay," she stressed.

"I appreciate it Sim, thank you. Goodnight."

"Goodnight."

Ahmed Kazemi. Ahmed Kazemi. Ahmed. Kazemi. His name only repeated itself in my head. Why hadn't I been paged by the agency? It probably didn't go through because of the poor connection here.

While letting the computer still buffer as it attempted to connect to the internet, I walked back outside to my car and unlocked the glove compartment. Inside, there was my gun, my badge, and underneath a few documents, my pager. But my pager had only one new notification from a few days ago,

Training re-certification seminar for Tuesday is cancelled because of ongoing investigations with recent hospital attack.

I put the pager back and locked the glove compartment once again. My only answers were going to come from that computer for now.

Though the internet connection was very slow, I was eventually able to access my email. Despite the time it took, I needed to see Jamal's email...to see that face. When I clicked on the inbox, the subject of his email was "TST 194 Security Notice" - a code indication that a partially identified terrorist was in hiding. I double clicked on the email and waited slowly as the page loaded, word by word.

The email read,

> *This terrorist has been identified as the key planner and executer in the bombings of Memorial Hospital that killed 132 people. The young man, estimated to be in his mid to late twenties, was last seen a few kilometers from the hospital six days ago on the day of the bombings. Please be cautious - he is most likely armed and dangerous. A warrant has been placed to arrest him, as long as he cooperates. His level of danger*

presents him with the possibility of a shoot on sight

case. Do not attempt to arrest him without additional

aid - he is trained in our defensive procedures and is

very capable of hurting or killing anyone in his way. If

you meet with any information, please contact your

supervisor.

I waited eagerly as the photo loaded.

This was the terrorist that was responsible for killing

Nima and so many others that were so close to my heart. I

prayed for the fastest arrest possible. Slowly, the picture was

starting to appear, loading from top to bottom. The online

connection was very slow, but I was willing to spend all day to

see the face of the man responsible for such a horrendous

attack. The faster I could identify him, the faster I could help

get justice for Nima and each of the innocent victims in that

hospital.

The heading of the picture had come through first.

Ahmed Kazemi was written in big, bold letters. After seeing

the name written out on the computer, it appeared

familiar...something a bit like Déjà Vu. I had seen this name before...for sure...but where? My memory brought me nothing but the feeling that I had seen this name in my past. I thought that the picture would perhaps jog my memory. As the image continued to load, I kept my eyes locked on the screen.

But my heart disregarded the photo as soon as I saw it - my mind yelled in shock...frustration, but my gut told me something wasn't right.

That wasn't Ahmed...that was Kabir.

It was a picture of Kabir - a very recent one too. He was the terrorist? Kabir? My brain began to explode in confusion - I tried to think clearly and practically, but nothing made sense to me. Kabir? It had to be some kind of mistake? But there was a connection between the description of Ahmed and the Kabir that was just a small walk away from me. Ahmed was last seen six days ago - I found Kabir on that road six days ago. Was that why he was beaten? Did someone identify him before we could and try to take justice into their own hands? It was making too much sense. But I wanted no sense of it to be real.

I couldn't accept any of it as true, emotionally. Never in my life had I felt so conflicted. Part of me, with the mindset from the scene of the bombing, wanted to pull out my gun and aim it at Kabir - the "Ahmed" from the email. But a greater part of me, with the mindset of laughter and love from the past few days, wanted to hold on to Kabir - to protect him from the very people who wanted revenge against him - people like me.

"It's only been six days Mandira," my brain kept screaming at me. "You have no clue who he truly is - he was too good to be true. He's a terrorist."

But he wasn't. Six days is all it took for me to know him. Crazy…but my heart told me that Kabir wasn't responsible. That Kabir was not a terrorist.

I shut off my computer and simply stared at the black screen. What the hell was going on? What should I do? Should I call the office? Should I let him get away based on the trust I've built on him in just six days? Six days. What the hell should I do?

Without even knowing what I could do, what I should do, I began to walk back to the cottage. Now I understood why Sim said that Jamal felt that the terrorist was a familiar face...they had seen each other in Delhi, as Kabir had mentioned before. But I still had no explanation for why the name Ahmed Kazemi seemed familiar to me. And that lack of an explanation was my source of hope. This had to be some kind of mistake. Ahmed Kazemi, whoever he was, must still be out there. People were looking for the wrong man. I wanted to believe that so much. So much.

I needed to look at Kabir - to see him - to see if there was someone in there that was different from the man I knew. But I had great faith in the Kabir I knew. I believed and trusted the Kabir I knew.

Unlocking the door to the cottage, I walked into complete darkness, aside from the fireplace that had a few gentle flames in the corner. As I was trying to find the switch, dim lights suddenly brightened the back patio, revealing a small round table covered in a black tablecloth with a dining set for two. There, Kabir was standing, wearing a navy-blue dress shirt and black pants. He looked so handsome. I tried to tell myself to pull away the trust that I had built in him. I tried. But my gut and heart shut those attempts down.

"I'm so sorry for being late Kabir - I got sidetracked with a phone call. I'm so sorry," I said as I closed the door behind me.

"No worries at all," he smiled.

"Everything looks so amazing."

Everything was set so beautifully. There was a small glass vase of red roses resting on the round table in the back patio and this wonderful scent of masala in the air.

"I see you can smell the food. Can you guess what's for dinner?"

"Hmm. Paneer?" I guessed after taking in the smell of the spices.

"You've gotten to know me so fast," he laughed as he placed the paneer on the table. "But like you've said, I've also gotten to know you. Your favorite..."

He lifted the cover off a ceramic dish, revealing a delicious looking pot of chicken biryani.

"How did you know?" I gasped. I was in awe and fear of him. But it was my heart and gut that seemed to be winning the battle.

"My grandma would always say, 'Kabir - the best way to a woman's heart is through her stomach. How do you think I fell in love with your grandfather?' And with that, my grandfather taught me how to make my grandmother's favorite - chicken biryani. She always said that the girl who could appreciate my cooking would be special. And I overheard you asking Madhu about chicken biryani," he laughed.

"You did all of this?"

"To the garnish on your plate," he said, smiling. "So, it's a win-win. I get my beautiful date and you get some of my special dishes."

"This is so incredible Kabir," I said as I put my hand over my mouth, impressed with everything he had done.

My mind was still being sidetracked by the recent information, but in all honesty, there was so much warmth and love in Kabir...I knew it...I just did. And everything was set up so beautifully. But what if he was lying to me? What if all this was his way to manipulate me...his way of hiding...surviving? But seeing him, I couldn't help but ignore those questions. Kabir was Kabir...the Kabir I've seen for the last week. That's all my heart was accepting...my brain was telling me otherwise. Slowly though, even my mind left the very last moments at the computer near the reception desk to solely be in that moment with Kabir.

I looked at him - he wasn't the Kabir from my email. He was the Kabir that sang to DDLJ tunes, the Kabir that loved paneer, the Kabir that couldn't fish, the Kabir that always had such a genuine charm.

I adored him.

He grabbed a hold of my hand and pulled out my chair. After I sat down, he too sat and began to place a large spoonful of chicken biryani on my plate.

He eased my stress - took away the shadows that lurked over my emotions. But I suddenly began to feel the weight of Nima's death again...I wanted to find her justice...but people saw her justice in the arrest...in the death of Kabir, even though I knew...I knew it was not him they were truly looking for.

"From your smile, I can tell you're enjoying the food, but there's pain in your eyes Mandira. What's wrong?"

For a moment, I paused. There was silence aside from the flickering flames of the fireplace.

"Oh nothing, nothing's wrong," I said as I moved the rice around my plate.

"Tell me. I know it's not nothing," he said as he gently held my hand. "If you're comfortable talking about it, I'm here to listen," he assured me.

"That explosion last week...132 people were killed. I knew so many of those people - one of them was my best friend. I don't know...I just get these thoughts back in my head from things that went on last week. I still feel the pain of that day...like a weight on my chest."

135

I tried to see if there was any change in his expression when I talked about the explosion. It did change, but to an expression of sincerity.

"Remember how I told you the other day that your goodness is your weakness and strength," said Kabir. "I think it's your weakness because I feel like you're someone that's so loving and giving to others that sometimes you forget to love and give to yourself. You take on the pain of others, their burdens and troubles, but you leave yours for last."

He held my hands in his and looked at me with so much love. So much genuine love.

"Don't forget to love yourself Mandira. Because you're a pretty great girl."

"You're a good man Kabir."

"You're the one that's a good human being Mandira." He pulled his chair in a bit closer.

"I've never met someone in my life who's been so understanding of me, and so quickly too. You're a beautiful woman Mandira, but what I love most about you is that your beauty radiates from who you are as a person. The way you seem to treat anyone around you. I have just seen the way you are with me and Madhu, but that's all I need to see to know how good you truly are."

Smiling and still holding my hand, he walked me over to the balcony.

"Look there," he said, pointing to a star in the sky. "You know how you said Zindagi said special things happen with the rain. My grandmother would also tell me that these beautiful bright stars were a special sign from Allah. See that one bright star over there - my grandmother used to call that Allah's eye because whenever it appeared in the sky, she knew that Allah was there, trying to show us that there was still goodness in the world. That star always appears on the toughest of days. I remember the night my grandmother passed away, my grandfather said it was the brightest it had ever been. And today, I think that star is even brighter. It's pointing to your goodness Mandira...because although goodness may be a weakness at times, I think it's your greatest strength. Someone who holds on to goodness when the world tries to push it away from them with pain and sorrow...that's someone special."

There, we simply gazed at the sky. Kabir's words reflected the pain I felt. I always have wanted to make everyone around me feel loved...to be good to everyone, but so many times, I had felt that the world didn't want me to feel that way. Kabir...Kabir was not a painful part of that world for me...but now, it seemed like the world was trying to take him away from me...to make him a part of that world that made me question my desire to hold on to the goodness that Kabir spoke of.

"It's something that makes me in awe of you...it's what makes me want to be a good man for you Mandira. Can I be that good man for you?"

Just as the moon began to hide behind the stars, there was a moment of beautiful silence between me and Kabir. He was beautiful - a beautiful man with a beautiful heart that would never hurt anyone. I trusted him. I just did.

Slowly, both of us leaned our heads toward each other. But just as our lips slightly touched, my mind began to pull me back. I loved him - I knew that and had no doubt about it anymore. But my mind kept telling me to hold myself back - to be careful. More than that though, I couldn't stand lying to him. He didn't know that there was a death warrant out for him - he didn't know that I was someone that would be responsible for carrying out such a death warrant. I turned my head downward as his lips kissed my cheek instead.

"I'm sorry Kabir - I...I can't. I...I'm sorry." I let go of his hand and walked away from him towards the door to the cottage. I didn't want to hurt him. I wanted to protect him.

"Mandira," he gently called out to me.

He grabbed a hold of my arm and gently pulled me away from the door, softly pressing my back against the outside wall that guarded the patio. He placed his hands lovingly around my head, moving the hair out of my face, stroking my cheek.

"Please don't go Mandira."

139

Our breathing became heavier.

"Kabir...I can't," I said as I looked to the ground. I wanted to kiss him...to hold him close and never let go, but my mind - that conflict - it was cutting in... pushing me away from him.

As both of us were standing, with my back to the wall, Kabir began to kiss me on the neck, down my chest, and slowly moved towards my stomach.

"Kabir..." I said softly as my breathing became deeper.

"Mandira - tell me to stop, and I'll stop," he said as his lips slowly made his way back up my body.

"But please don't tell me that you don't love me. I see the love in your eyes - do you know how? Because your eyes mirror mine Mandira. I love you and I never want to let you go."

His lips met mine again.

"I love you Mandira," he whispered as his lips touched mine.

I kissed him, and instead of telling him that I didn't love him, I told him that I did.

Slowly, I unbuttoned his shirt and traced my lips on the scars on his chest as he held me close and ran his fingers through my hair.

We continued to kiss, and gently, he carried me to the bed and laid me down. I loved him...and I didn't want to let go.

Chapter 6

The next morning, I woke up in his shirt with the rays of the sun on my face. As I was just starting to sit up in bed, Kabir, smiling, walked towards the bedside holding two cups of coffee. His shirt was still off, and the sun seemed to outline the defined muscles of his body. He was definitely a handsome man, but beyond that, he was a good human being.

I had always been a person that valued the mind over the heart. I never believed it when people said that their heart guided them to where they were. But for the first time in my life, I felt my heart speaking over my mind...and I wanted to hold on to that feeling. My mind was considering all of the accusations and warrants against him - but my heart made me feel like everyone else was so wrong about this man. If only they could know the genuine human being that he was. But where had all this information gone wrong? Where did the name Ahmed Kazemi come from? Where did the accusations sprout from?

"Good morning Mandira," he whispered.

"Good morning Kabir," I whispered. "Thank you," I said as he gave me some coffee.

We looked at each other with so much love, so much admiration, and so much respect. Kabir just had this ability to bring me into a sense of ease and comfort. Every time I was around him, I felt like my worries gradually faded.

"I never thought that I could fall in love with a man so fast."

He grabbed another shirt that was sitting on the side table and began to button it back on.

"I knew I would fall in love with you the moment I met you," he said with a sweet laugh.

We kissed again...the taste of fresh coffee on both of our lips.

"Kabir, can I ask you something?"

"Of course."

"Do you trust me?"

"More than I trust myself," he said as he put his coffee cup on the bedside table.

"I need to tell you something...but I need you to keep trusting me okay?"

"What's wrong Mandira?" he said as he lovingly placed his hand around my face. I put my hand on top of his and squeezed tightly, scared by what I was going to tell him. Love can be very blind, but this time, I hoped the world was making an exception.

"Yesterday, my brother sent me the news that the police have identified who they believe is the other terrorist in the explosion that happened at that hospital."

"That's great - have they found him yet?"

His question was so incredibly sincere. He had no clue it was him. There was nothing he was hiding.

"No... but I have...Kabir - they've identified the terrorist as you."

Kabir sat back, moving his hand from my face and into my lap, still holding my hand.

145

"What?" he said with shock.

"They have a warrant for your arrest and they've placed you on the shoot on sight list if it comes to that for them. It's all over the news."

His shocked face and posture remained stagnant.

"Mandira - I promise you - I'm innocent. I swear Mandira on my life. I know that I can't remember much of what happened to me...but I know - I know that I would never even think of hurting someone. Please Mandira...trust me," he said as he held my hand tighter.

"I trust you Kabir. I promise you...we'll figure this out as soon as we can. Nobody knows you're with me...nobody but Madhu knows that you are here with me, and Madhu does not know anything about this either," I assured him.

"Do you think this might be a reason I was beaten the night you found me?"

"I do. Someone is trying to put this on you...I don't know who...but someone is definitely targeting you for the blame."

Suddenly, there was a change in Kabir's expression.

"Mandira - I've heard about the things they do to people that shelter or protect terrorists. If they find out that you're with me...I want you to report me Mandira - I don't want them to hurt you."

I put my hand around his face, assuring him to not worry.

"You're not a terrorist Kabir. You're a good man. A great man. No one can take that away from you. As much as the police and the media and the public who've been fed this information will try to degrade the man that you are, no one can take away the truth. Trust me Kabir. Trust me."

"I trust you."

***

This evening seemed much more silent and dark than the previous nights. No stars, no rain, nothing besides a few cricket chirps here and there. Kabir and I hadn't talked about the recent news since this morning. We were both trying to wrap our heads around what was going on and trying to stay calm at the same time.

I spent most of my time near the reception desk today, trying to see if there was any more information. But nothing was new, except for the fact that Kabir's picture had been made public within the last few hours. It was broadcasted on all televisions, in the newspapers, everywhere. This isolated cottage area seemed to be his only safe haven...with such little access to the internet, no one here was bound to know about what was going on in the outside world.

Around 11:00 p.m., I decided to head back to the cottages. Before I even opened the door, I could see Kabir through the window. He had taken off his shirt and was looking at himself in the mirror. His hands were tracing the scars on his body, the gashes in his skin. He had this expression of confusion, but even more so of sorrow. I could feel his confusion...his sorrow. He wasn't the Kabir from the news - he was my Kabir.

Just as I was unlocking the cottage door, I thought I heard a very faint sound from the outside, but I couldn't tell what it was or where exactly it was coming from. At first, I thought it could have been the random ringing in my ears - it's something I've experienced on and off since the night of the explosion that killed Zindagi, but I usually didn't notice it unless there was complete silence in my surroundings.

Just as I was about to pass it off as nothing, I heard the sound again - this time louder and distinguished. It sounded like a child, but that's all I could make of it. I closed my eyes and listened carefully to focus on where the sound was coming from.

Within seconds, I heard it again. It was coming from the cottage below ours - the one with the faint glow from the window that was visible from our own cottage. I walked to the side of our cottage to try to get a better look, but the cottage was a bit too far to see anything clearly.

I hadn't seen a single family on this property since we had arrived - it was just me, Kabir, Madhu, and Arbazz - that's

149

it. I hadn't even seen Arbazz since the first night. But someone was there. Something felt very wrong.

Carefully, I walked down the hill that led to the other cottage. There was no path - just bushes and uncut grass that grew taller the farther downhill I got. After taking less than ten steps closer, I figured out what the sound was - it was the voice of a young girl, and her tone of voice was frantic and frightened.

"Help us, please! Somebody! Please! Plea..." she cried. Her voice broke into tears towards the end.

I began to run towards that cottage and the closer I got, the more scared I began to feel about what I would see.

Unlike our cottage, this cottage was much smaller and had only one window, from where the dim lighting came. The roof looked like it was caving in and the once white walls were now dripped in mud and dirt that had blown in from the wind and rain. The window was shattered with jagged pieces of glass sticking out of the frames crossed with the webs of spiders. But it's the moment I looked passed that broken glass that I will never forget.

The shock of what I was seeing made me feel sick - I covered my mouth with my trembling hands - I felt like I was going to throw up.

Inside, there was a young girl, perhaps thirteen or fourteen years old. She was lying on a dirty bed that was in the center of the room with half-dead rose petals dispersed on it and around the floor. Her hands were tied with thick rope to the bed stands, her eyes were blackened, and her clothes were stained in blood. Tears were running down her cheeks and desperation and defeat covered her face.

I ran to the front door, but the door had a lock on it that was tightly and awkwardly placed on the knob. I knew how to pick a lock, but I needed to loosen it from the door. I decided to try something new. I had learned about it in some of my previous training, but I had never really tried it.

I took off my belt, which had a small metal buckle on the front, and wrapped the belt around my shoe, with the metal sticking out at the bottom. Holding the two ends of the belt, I did a snap kick at the knob, using the metal buckle to hit the lock. It took me three tries, but the chain finally chipped to the extent that I could more easily pick the lock. I pulled out a hair pin and within a few seconds, was able to get the door open.

The inside smell of the cottage hit me immediately - it was a pungent mixture of sweat, blood, and semen. It almost reminded me of the smell of death that I've encountered so many times on the job. There was also a strong stench of alcohol - the same hard liquor smell that Arbazz had on that very first night.

Right away, I met the eyes of the young girl on the bed - her eyes were filled with tears and blood. Her skin was pale, and parts of her body were swollen, especially her lower abdomen and parts around her neck.

I quickly ran to her side and began to untie the many knots that strapped her to the bed. The rope was tied very tightly - the more I loosened it, the more visible the scars on her wrists had become from being tied up for so long. When I untied the final set of rope knots, she fell into my arms and began to cry. I could feel her tears - the weight and pain that they carried.

I held her in my arms for a few moments - she deserved so much to be loved and taken care of. I couldn't help but cry as well. When she sat back, my arms still around her, I looked at her - she had been so brutally abused that her eyes conveyed emptiness and pain. A broken necklace with a pendant of the sun was hanging off her neck - this was Madhu's sister.

"Rh...Rhe..." she moaned. She was trying to tell me something, but the fear inside of her drowned her voice out with tears. I've never seen someone so scared before.

Suddenly, and with urgency, she kept on repeating, "Rhea...Rhea is somewhere...please ma'am...help me find Rhea...she's somewhere here."

"Who's Rhea? What happened? Sweetheart, where is she?"

"I...I don't know ma'am." She started to cry again. I gently held her face in my hands, wiping away her tears, even though I couldn't stop mine.

"Don't worry - we'll find her. Meera?"

She nodded gently while emptiness continued to capture her emotions.

"Meera - don't worry, we'll find Rhea. I'm going to take you up to my cottage and get you to a hospi-"

"I'll be fine - please help me find Rhea. She needs help. She's here - I don't know where, but she's in here," she said with panicked urgency.

"Okay Meera. There's a man in the cottage on the hill - I need you to go there and get that man - his name is Kabir...he will help you...he's with me okay. I'm going to look for Rhea - Kabir won't hurt you, I promise."

"Ma'am...please find Rhea...she...she's like my little sister - she's so young and I...I don't know...I don't know what Arbazz has done to her."

"We'll find her - I promise you - we will find her. I need you to stay strong Meera...for you and for Rhea. Okay?"

With tears continuously streaming down her cheeks, she gently nodded and stood up. She hugged me once more, and I held her closely - I so badly wanted to take away her pain - she was so young.

She then slowly made her way out the door towards our cottage. I wanted to get Kabir...Meera looked like she was in so much pain. But she insisted that I look for Rhea...and that Arbazz would be back soon.

I began to search frantically for Rhea - I wasn't even sure if she was truly there. The cottage was much smaller, but the smell was blinding and made it much more difficult to make my way around. I checked the bathroom, the back patio, and under the bed. There was no sign of Rhea. After a few minutes, I thought that Rhea must be somewhere else. There was only one last spot I had not checked: a small closet - no more than a meter tall and wide. With my mind trying to adjust to what I might find inside, I pulled open the closet door and was devastated with what I saw.

It was a toddler - not even close to being more than three years old. Her eyes were closed, almost like she was sleeping. She was half-naked with blood patches on her body and her hair disheveled. Hanging off her neck was a small broken necklace that had a small medallion with the letter 'R' engraved into it.

I couldn't mentally accept what I was seeing. I lost control of all of my emotions - I sobbed and became filled with rage and anger. Arbazz...his empty bottles surrounded Rhea in the closet - all I wanted to do was to stab Arbazz. How could he do this to a child?

I carried her out of the closet - her body was so light and frail. Her body was much more heavily bruised, and her skin was very cool to the touch. She had a long-slanted cut on her right cheek, just like what I had seen on Meera. I laid her gently on the floor...I didn't even think she could survive,

156

especially being as young as she was. But I didn't want to lose hope - I couldn't lose hope on her.

I checked her breathing and pulse - she was still alive, though it was very possible that she could lose her life at any moment. She had a deep wound on her waist that itself was somewhat healed but looked partially infected. There was a small jug of water, so I grabbed it and gently washed away some of the dirt that surrounded some of the cuts on her body as I tried to process my own shock. Deep down, I felt that Rhea wasn't going to survive. The least I could do for her was to clean her wounds.

Just as I was doing that, Arbazz came from behind, placed a hand over my mouth, lifted me, and pushed me against the wall. I didn't even hear him come inside. For a second, I was able to push myself away from his face. In that second, I called out to Kabir for help with the hope that Kabir could somehow hear me, but Arbazz's grip only got tighter.

Arbazz with more force pressed his hands over my mouth and began to laugh crudely. With his hand still over my mouth, he pulled a small knife out of his pant pocket and cut

my face across my right cheek. I yelled in pain, but all that

could be heard was a small muffled sound because of his

hands. He carefully placed the knife back into his pocket, but

he kept his eyes locked on me. He then placed his tongue

where he had cut me, and soon, my blood covered his lips,

while the salty sweat from his face painfully stung me.

Arbazz was a strong man. Despite everything I knew

about self-defense, nothing worked on him. He was drunk and

angry - a fatal combination for someone in his hands. Without

a problem and with one hand still over my mouth, he forced

me onto the same dirty bed that I had just untied Meera from.

"Mandira - I've waited for this moment since I met you.

I was planning on coming after you soon, but everything

seemed to work out - you even came to my own cottage.

Sorry. I should have done this to you sooner. It's a shame that

Kabir got to have you before I did - but I'll say sorry for him

too. I don't think he could satisfy you the way I can. I don't

think anyone can satisfy you like I can - such a beautiful

woman like you," he said as he tightly pinched my cheeks under his grip. "I tried it with the girls, but it was very difficult. It will be much easier for me to get myself into you. Their bodies are just too small and immature, especially of that one...uh...Reema? No...uh...yeah...Rhea."

I wanted to kill him.

He sat on top of me, and he moved his hands from my mouth to my throat, gripping tightly around my neck. I was losing my ability to breathe - he was trying to make me lose consciousness.

Trying to get him to stop strangling me was useless, especially with his strength. I decided to reach for his knife - I just needed to get a hold of his pant pocket, but he was sitting just a bit too low on my abdomen for me to reach it. I needed him to move his body upwards toward my chest. So I grabbed his shirt collar and pulled him closer to me. His hands were still gripping my neck, and his lips were now closer to mine, but he moved up on my body just enough for me to reach his pocket.

Before I grabbed the knife, he pressed his bloody lips to mine. It was my own blood on his lips that I tasted. As he started to unbutton my shirt and press his lips onto my breasts, I pulled the knife out of his pocket and pushed it directly into his lower abdomen. He yelled in pain and immediately, his hands moved from my neck to his bleeding wound. My breathing began to stabilize as soon as I could get a complete breath of air. While he was still putting pressure to his own wound, I called out to Kabir. I only had a few seconds, and Kabir was my only hope. Arbazz was still sitting on top of me and I couldn't get him off. I was able to call out to Kabir twice, but before I could call out to him again, Arbazz forced his lips against mine to keep me quiet.

"You need to stop this game Mandira - forget Kabir," he said as he bit my lip. "Come on - say my name Mandira. Arbazz. Say it Mandira. Arba…"

Again, he forced his lips to mine, and was soon attempting to force his body into mine. I tried to push him off, but again, his body weighed too much. I felt like my bones

160

were soon going to crack under him. I prepared myself for what he was planning to do.

Suddenly, his weight was lifted off me and all I could see at first was Arbazz's body getting thrown off the bed, his head bashed against the wall. As Arbazz was collapsed on the floor, Kabir stood above him, with his hands in tight fists but his face in worry. Right behind him, Meera stood, with Madhu holding her to prevent her from collapsing.

Meera's face stood blank, though Madhu's screamed silently in sorrow and rage. Arbazz got up and grabbed on to Kabir, but Kabir was able to beat Arbazz enough to push Arbazz back to the floor and keep him there. While Kabir was keeping Arbazz down, I grabbed Arbazz's car keys from his pocket and rushed to get Rhea. She was left exactly where she was when Arbazz pulled me away from her, but her skin had grown paler. I took her into my arms and ran out the door to put her into the car, calling out to Meera and Madhu to follow me. Rhea felt so unimaginably fragile - the run to the car on the hill was a difficult one.

I placed Rhea in the back seat as softly as I could. I grabbed a small pillow, which I placed beneath her head to ensure better body stabilization for her, along with some blankets to help cushion her body. I secured her to the seat with two seatbelts, but I overextended the seatbelts to ensure that they didn't tighten around her body. Once Meera and Madhu were in the car, I got into the driver's seat and sped the car downhill towards Arbazz's cottage. We needed to get out of here as soon as possible.

"Kabir! Get in the car - we need to leave!"

I got a quick glimpse of Arbazz - it seemed like he had passed out as a result of his drunkenness and Kabir's beating.

Leaving Arbazz where he was, Kabir ran towards the car. With Kabir sitting in the passenger's seat and Madhu sitting between Meera and Rhea in the back seat, I drove the car as fast as I could out of the property.

***

About an hour into the drive, I decided to stop the car and check on the girls. There were many broken branches and debris covering the roads from the recent storms, making the drive much more arduous. The hospital was still too far - I needed to make sure that they had at least been better stabilized and as comfortable as they could be.

Kabir helped me get my medical supplies that I had grabbed before we left from the trunk of the car as I attempted to clean some of the wounds, especially the ones that had started to become infected on Rhea. As I opened the back door, all I could notice was the mutual blankness across Meera and Rhea's face. Madhu held them both lovingly, with tears running without end. He looked up at me in sorrow - the kind of sorrow I had felt with Nima...that something could have been done to prevent this.

"Madhu," I said softly as I patted his shoulder to comfort him as he held on to both of their hands. Slowly, Kabir came inside the back seat to carry Rhea in his arms, so that it would be easier for me to treat her.

"Do you know Rhea? Where she's from? Who her parents are?"

"I don't know Di…" He broke down into tears. I embraced him, trying to console him, but he was inconsolable. "How could someone do this to them? They're both so young - I should have done something...I should have known about…"

"Madhu," I sighed. "Don't put any of this on yourself."

I could feel his pain and I could understand some of his guilt. I wanted him to remove himself from that - he didn't deserve to have to face such a situation ever...but it made it worse that he was only sixteen years old.

I looked at Kabir, his face with sorrow as well. He was holding Rhea in his arms, and as he looked down at her small, crumbling body, he too had tears.

"Madhu - you are the best brother a person could ask for...the way you take care of your sister - only someone who carries the heart of God can do that the way you do," said Kabir as he looked directly at Madhu, who held his face in his hands. "Remember this Madhu...you did everything you could and can do to protect her. Sometimes, there are moments in our lives, no matter how hard we try, that will beat us before we can beat them."

"How much he must have hurt her? She has so many dreams...so much in her heart to help others..." cried Madhu.

"You're her strength Madhu," I said, "just as she is yours."

"And the other little girl...how could someone do that ... how could someone do something like that?" he asked as he looked up at me.

"I don't think I'll ever know the answer to that Madhu," I said sorrowfully.

I embraced him tightly. And he held on even tighter. He was feeling the pain of a nightmare that he couldn't wake up from, and that shattered my heart.

Gently, I let go of Madhu and asked for his help to hold Meera up a little bit. I first cared for Meera's wounds...they were not as deep and were more easily cleaned. The faster I could clean up her wounds, the more rest she could get. Her skin was cold and blue...her beatings had been taking a huge toll on her body. Her body was nothing but bruises...Arbazz must have tried to beat her to death from what the injuries on her body showed.

As I cleaned off some of the blood that dripped on her skin, she looked at me with blank eyes...they looked much different from when I had first found her on that bed.

It seemed that, in that moment, she had been alive for the sake of Rhea...her eyes were then frantically trying to save Rhea. But now...she seemed to have lost all thoughts...all life. She seemed to be here, alive...for the sole sake of Rhea. She wasn't responsive...she had no expression...nothing but emptiness covered her face...and it was all because of the trauma she had experienced.

Volunteering at the hospital, I've seen girls who have just come out of abuse with an extent of blankness in their expression due to shock...but never had I seen it to the extent I saw it in Meera...and it devastated me in a way that words can never...and will never describe.

I told her to get some rest, to relax the stiffness in her body if she could...she remained exactly how she was...rigid and lost in emptiness.

I then walked over to Kabir, who held Rhea in his arms. I placed a few blankets on the floor and Kabir gently laid Rhea down on the ground so that I could have enough space to treat some of Rhea's wounds.

She still had that sleeping look on her face...almost like she was dreaming. There was no pain, no sorrow, nothing but serenity on her face. Her body told me otherwise.

Arbazz had cut so deeply into her body...I could see her bare bone in her right leg. He had ripped the flesh right off her. Her skin was turning a darker shade of blue. There was no doubt in my mind that she had severe internal bleeding, and there was nothing I could do.

She had a pulse, but it was a fading one. I knew I couldn't save her - she was in God's hands now. And I think that's where her dream-like expression came from...her pain was gone...she was free from it. But I didn't want her to die with all of her open wounds and with all the dirt that covered her body. I wanted her to live her last moments with the dignity and love she deserved.

Kabir could tell from the look of my eyes that I didn't feel like Rhea could survive. He grabbed a bottle of water from the car and helped me clean Rhea's body of the dirt and blood that ran down her skin. We took care of her in painful silence - we knew she wouldn't be with us in just a few moments.

Just as Kabir was cleaning off her last wound, I took her necklace out of my pocket. I looked at the little cracked 'R' engraved into it - I had picked it up on our way out of that cottage. I could feel tears streaming down my cheeks...I was holding on to the one thing that Rhea owned.

She was stripped of everything, even before she could begin to understand anything. This necklace was the last thing that she had - she barely even had a piece of clothing on her. Life is so incredibly fragile...I've learned that over the years, but tonight, I felt like hope was just as fragile.

I put the broken necklace in her hands and cradled her small fingers around it. Kabir wrapped her body in a blanket as I moved the hair out of her face. She was gone.

Kabir helped me lay her in the back seat comfortably. We wanted to take her to a hospital and to find out if she had a family or someone that could perform final rites for her. Meera continued to sit right with Rhea, holding her hand, never once letting go. And for the first time in my life, I witnessed death in someone who was still physically alive. Meera was gone too - she wasn't responsive, and her eyes were blank. Arbazz had killed her. I wanted to hold on to my hope for her, but I'll never forget that look in her eyes. The look that someone had abused her to the extent of mental death. Hope was even more fragile than I could have ever imagined.

Just as I was about to get back in the car to drive again, I suddenly felt extremely light-headed and collapsed near the back tire of the car. Kabir caught me before I hit the ground, laid me upright against the tire, and grabbed another bottle of water. He came to my side, helped me hold the bottle in my hand as I drank, and held my face in his hands, wiping the blood off my lips with his thumb.

"Mandira...are you alright?" he asked as he held me up gently.

"Just feeling a bit light-headed," I responded with a shaky voice.

Suddenly, he pressed his hand against my lower right abdomen.

"You're losing blood Mandira."

I looked down to realize that I had a deep gash in my side. I hadn't even realized that Arbazz had stabbed me. There was no pain but Kabir was right - I was losing blood. I placed my hand on his as he continued to put pressure on my wound. I leaned my head back on the side of the car. Kabir quickly ripped off a part of a blanket and used it to help slow down my blood loss.

"Mandira, I need to get you to a hospital," he said as he wrapped my wound.

"Just a few minutes Kabir," I said as I took a heavy breath. "I just need a few minutes."

He kept his hand pressed against my side and held his other hand over mine, which was resting on the floor.

Sitting in silence, leaning against the car, a memory came back into my thoughts.

"Five months ago," I said as I swallowed. "I met this little boy named Ayan. He had come to the hospital on his own...his eyes were burned and blistered. Someone had poured acid into his eyes. They were trying to get more profit out of his begging on the streets...so they blinded him. He was only seven years old. And he had gone through so much...he was an orphan, was separated from his only brother, and was raped by the very man that he said blinded him. Yet he somehow always...always had this smile on his face," I said while looking out at the dark sky. I could still feel the tears coming down my cheeks.

"He told me that first night I met him that what made him stay smiling was the hope that one day things would get

171

better," I groaned softly as I felt a jolt of pain in my abdomen. "The hope that he would be able to see his six-year-old brother again. And you know…he stayed smiling. Always did. The most hope I've ever seen in a human being before. And ever since he came to that hospital, he worked alongside me. Helped me treat the kids that came through those doors. Sat down with them and played. Talked and laughed all the time. Such a beautiful soul. But one day, that man that had blinded him," I sighed. "He somehow found out that Ayan was staying with me," I said as I swallowed again taking a deep breath. "And I came home one evening to see Ayan on my kitchen floor, shot six times. Six times...not even animals are treated with such brutality. I held that little boy in my arms during his last moments, and even then, he looked up at me and he smiled. His last words to me... 'I can see him. I see him.' And then, he was gone." I closed my eyes for a moment, trying to hold off the jabbing pains in my chest.

"It was raining that day too," I added. "And with that rain, I felt that all God was telling me was that he hated me.

And in that moment, I hated him. I hated him for taking away so much goodness from the world. I hated him for allowing kids like Ayan to have to face so much pain. I hated him for punishing the innocent. I hated him," I emphasized. "But about a week later, I received news from a local children's home. A six-year-old boy named Aarahan had passed away about two weeks before because of a brain tumor that was caught too late. The children's home was trying to see if they could find his brother - Ayan. I think that's who Ayan saw when he said that he could see someone - Aarahan."

Kabir ripped the bottom part of my shirt and grabbed another cloth to press against my wound.

"I thought that was God's way of telling me that he didn't hate me...that he was telling me that things happen for a reason, even if the reason makes no sense to us. But tonight, I can't help but feel that sense of hatred again. And I don't want to feel that way...I don't, but I do. Zindagi would always say this quote from the Bible - 'God can bring peace to your past, purpose to your present, and hope to your future.' But where is that hope? I'm fearful that my sense of hope in life is disappearing Kabir."

"There's a quote in Arabic that says, 'Your faith has to be greater than your fear.' And as a kid, there were times when I felt like my fears were much stronger than my faith...I felt like Allah was placing me with so much pain and so many burdens. I remember coming home with a black eye from school to my grandfather. I had been beaten for being a Muslim...the kids would call me a terrorist and said that my family had moved from Pakistan with only the desire to kill as many Indians as we could. I can understand your feeling of hate towards God...my two cousins, who were like older brothers to me, were killed at the Pakistan and Indian border because of their Muslim background. I felt hatred towards Allah because I felt like he was taking away the people I loved because they loved him," said Kabir, biting his lip in anguish. "I remember telling my grandfather that I didn't want to be a Muslim anymore...that I was scared to be a Muslim. But he told me to only stop being a Muslim if I didn't believe in Allah on my own terms...not based on what others believed. And I believed in Allah and the hope for life as a Muslim when I separated myself from the pain that those kids would bring me." He gently pressed against my abdomen to help slow down my blood loss as he reached for some gauze and bandages.

"In the Quran, there's another verse that says, 'Allah does not burden a soul beyond that it can bear.' And I know that your soul is incredible," he said as he looked into my eyes. "Hold on to that hope Mandira...because hope is what makes life worth living, especially when we're in the roughest of times. I still have the fear that my background has the risk of bringing me down...it's what's happening now in the news. I'm being labeled a terrorist again...but my faith is stronger than that fear...my faith in you is stronger than the fears that the world seems to throw at me. Don't let go of your hope Mandira."

Kabir held my hand tightly.

"We will get Rhea and Meera the justice they deserve," he assured me.

These words sounded so familiar...Jamal had said the same thing in terms of getting justice for Nima. I just didn't know when or how that justice would come. All I could do in the moment was believe that somehow, it would.

Chapter 7

For kilometers, the only thing visible outside was the charcoal sky above the dirt road. Kabir drove the rest of the way because of the fatigue that I had felt as a result of the amount of blood I had lost. After almost two more hours of driving, we finally reached a hospital. It was much larger than the one I had worked at and its bright white lights shone into the dark night.

Our car was parked at a distance. I could see an ambulance pulling up to the entrance and several cars parked around the area. But our car was hidden in the shadows, away from the eyes of others.

"Kabir, you need to stay in the car," I groaned.

"Mandira...you can't go in on your own," he said with concern.

"Kabir...if someone recognizes you, there's a good chance they will kill you. Please, for me, stay in the car. I'll be back soon."

"And the girls?"

"I will take them inside...I can't risk losing you Kabir...I can't. And Madhu is here...he'll help me."

Slowly, I made my way out of the car. Madhu helped me get out and opened the back door of the car. He took Rhea into his arms and gently, I eased Meera out of the car as well. I began to feel light-headed again, and after taking just a few steps out of the car, collapsed to my knees. Kabir ran to my side and helped me up.

"I'm coming with you Mandira," said Kabir as he helped me stand.

"Kabi-"

"You've done everything to help me...let me help you Mandira," he said sternly.

As we walked into the hospital, two nurses rushed to our side. They pulled up a wheelchair for Meera and grabbed a gurney to rest Rhea on. I told Madhu to stay with Meera.

"Let's get you a wheelchair and checked out as well," said a nurse as he motioned at my stab wound.

"I'll be fine for now - I need to make sure the girls are taken care of first," I said as I leaned my arm against a counter.

As doctors rolled the gurney with Rhea around the corner, Kabir and I waited in the hope that the hospital could access her records to see if she did have a family or someone that had been looking for her.

While I was sitting in the waiting room, I noticed a security guard in the corner with an expression of suspicion across his face. Kabir was filling out some paperwork at the front desk while I was trying to stay conscious and stop thinking about the pain in my abdomen. Before I could see if there was any greater suspicion in the eyes of the guard, a woman who was sitting next to me nudged my arm as she kept her eyes on the newspaper in her hands.

"These crazy people - Muslims. I'm telling you - they're all monsters," she said waving her paper. "Can't trust a single one. Hear about that attack at the hospital recently? Disgusting pigs!" she exclaimed.

"I think that there's good and bad among all kinds of people," I said in response. "There are good Muslims out there, just like there are good Hindus, Christians, and Atheists out there."

"You have to be in love with one to say bullshit like that," she responded with irritation. "Foolishness!" she exclaimed.

I looked back at the security guard. When I looked at him, he looked away, but when I looked away, from the corner of my eye, I could see him scanning Kabir. I slowly got up and approached Kabir.

"Kabir - keep your head down."

"What's wrong Mandira?" he asked while putting down his pen.

"People are starting to recognize you. If someone makes the connection -"

"Kabir and Mandira, you can come in and meet with the doctor now," said a nurse out loud.

When the nurse called for us, the security guard seemed to nudge his suspicion off as a mistake. To the world, it wasn't a man named Kabir who was responsible for the recent attack.

"Hello Mandira and..." said Maria as she looked at Kabir.

"Kabir," he said. "Nice to meet you Dr…"
Kabir held out his hand.

"Hi Kabir - nice to meet you." She held her hand out to shake Kabir's hand. "I'm Dr. Ahuja, but you can call me Maria."

"Nice to meet you Maria. You two know each other?" asked Kabir as he looked at me and back to Maria.

"Yeah - she's a childhood friend of mine from Church back home," I said as I gently smiled and patted her back.

Maria gently smiled and squeezed my hand out of love.

"There was no way to save Rhea unfortunately," said Maria as her smile quickly faded. "Her injuries were too severe. She suffered from intense internal bleeding. I am deeply sorry."

"Me too," said Kabir. "She was so young."

"Have you been able to find any previous medical reports for her? Any family members she may have?" I asked.

"We have her mother on file, but I'm sad to say she passed away a few years ago from a drug overdose. Other than that, we don't have any of her relatives noted in our documents," said Maria regretfully.

"Are we allowed to sign off for her, Maria?" I asked. "We don't want to leave her without anyone to do her final rites."

"It's against hospital policy for us to let patients be released to people other than primary relatives. But for you, I'll absolutely try to see what we can do."

"Thanks Maria."

"Of course," she nodded.

"And Meera?" asked Kabir.

"Meera is physically in much better condition, but she's facing a lot of psychological shock. As of now, she's completely unresponsive," said Maria sorrowfully. "Her mind is somewhere else. It's something that happens when someone undergoes an especially difficult experience of abuse. A common way for some people to escape their abuse is to mentally escape when they physically can't."

"I've worked with so many people who've been abused so brutally, but I've never seen someone in her condition before," I added.

"I agree - I've never seen this extreme of a response before," said Maria. "Her abuser really hurt her."

"Is there anything else we can do to help?" asked Kabir.

"As of now, the only option we have for Meera is physical therapy and to carry out some additional psychiatric tests to determine if we can find a proper treatment for her. Her mental health is what's most important right now - and I can't figure out how long it will take for her to regain a sense of mental stability again. And the costs of these treatments can really add up. Do you know her parents?"

"We can take care of the costs," said Kabir without hesitation.

"Absolutely - we'll take care of the costs," I repeated. "Meera's parents - they're not in her life anymore. But she has an older brother - he's that young boy in the lobby," I said as I pointed to Madhu who was looking out the window.

"The one with a waiter's uniform on?" asked Maria.

"Yes," I confirmed.

"He looks so young...how old is he?"

"He's sixteen, but he's a strong and mature kid with a really good heart. He's the one that takes care of Meera," said Kabir.

"Poor kid. Seems so sweet."

"He really is," I said as I looked at Madhu. "I can't imagine how he's feeling."

My focus quickly shifted to the security officer again. I could feel him staring at us. This time he was looking more closely at Kabir, and his look of suspicion seemed to transition into confirmation.

"Hey Mandira - you look a bit pale," said Maria as she looked at my face with concern. "Are you alright?"

"Yeah," I uttered while trying to look at the officer.

"Mandira - your wounds," said Kabir with concern as well.

"I'll be fine Kabir...I can wait for now," I told him.

I was focused on trying to figure out what this guard was thinking.

"Mandira, I can't let you risk your health - you've been cut deeply - you need to get treated," said Kabir earnestly.

I could see the guard starting to put his hand over his gun and walk towards us.

"Mandira - let me get that treated for you," added Maria after she took a closer look of where I had been stabbed.

"Thanks Maria, but I'm fine," I said again.

"Mandir-" said Kabir.

"Kabir - we need to leave," I said, cutting him off.

Kabir's picture suddenly appeared on the waiting room television. The guard was quick to make the connection. He grabbed a hold of his gun, and within seconds, yelled for everyone to step aside.

"Keep your hands up Ahmed," shouted the guard. His gun pointed directly at Kabir.

"We need to go," I whispered to Kabir from where I was standing.

I could see fear spread across Maria's face as she connected the photo on the news to Kabir.

"Maria - he's not dangerous. They're looking for the wrong guy. You need to trust me," I said with the hope that she would listen.

"Mandira - just follow the guard's directions. I don't want you to get killed - he will shoot if you try to run with Kabir," she whispered back while keeping her hands raised.

"It's a risk I'll take - please keep Rhea's body safe here and take care of Meera. I'll be back," I whispered to her. "Kabir!" I yelled as I pulled my gun out. I wasn't going to shoot the guard. But I wasn't going to let him shoot Kabir either.

Kabir grabbed my hand, and both of us ran through the hospital lobby. Everyone else got down as Kabir and I evaded the bullets that were coming at us continuously. I caught Madhu's eye as we were running, and he immediately understood that I wanted him to stay in this hospital with Meera and out of the danger that Kabir and I would bring to him. He had a confused expression on his face. Kabir and I never told him about the allegations, but, at the same time, I could tell that he believed in Kabir's innocence just as much as I did.

As we were running towards our car that was parked in the back of the lot, bullets flew past us just barely and one grazed across Kabir's arm. I quickly turned to see if the guard was slowing down. But he was still running and shooting. I pulled my trigger, shooting him in the knee to keep him far enough from us. He then stopped running towards us, but with his phone to his ear and a distressed expression on his face, it was clear that he was calling for backup.

I threw my keys to Kabir - I felt too light-headed to drive. Kabir and I got into the car, and quickly, I could hear the engine of our car roaring. We drove out into the darkness once again, attempting to catch our breath.

"Are you okay Mandira?" asked Kabir as he reached out to me with one hand.

"Yeah. I'll be fine." I pressed my hand against the large gash in my abdomen and took deep breaths to try to reduce the pain.

"Where did you get that gun?" he asked with a surprised look on his face.

"I'm a police officer Kabir," I said as I caught my breath. "An undercover agent. I might have forgotten to mention that," I said as I wiped the sweat off my face.

"Yeah, I think you did," he said in shock as he caught his breath and pressed on the accelerator. "You're bleeding more heavily now."

I looked down and realized that he was right. A bullet had managed to hit me right where I had been stabbed...and somehow, I hadn't even noticed that I had been shot. How could I have not noticed that I had been shot? Within moments, I began to feel dizzy and slowly, I became unresponsive.

"Mandira...stay with me Mandira. I'm pulling over...please stay with me Mandira," pleaded Kabir.

He pulled the car over to the side and reached over to look at my injury. He applied greater pressure and poured some cool water over my face. The cold water helped wake me up a little bit, but I still felt dizzy. Kabir held my face in his arms, and I could hear his voice eagerly trying to keep me from going unconscious.

"I'm taking you back to that hospital," I could hear him say.

There was no sign of anyone but me and him on the empty road once again. But suddenly, from nowhere, two bright police headlights appeared from the opposite direction. And those headlights got brighter and bigger, faster and closer.

.

Chapter 8

I was beginning to regain consciousness and all I could think about was how Mandira was doing...if she was okay. But when I turned my head to the passenger's seat, she was gone. Her seat belt had been raggedly cut off and only blood was left on her side of the car. Surrounded by broken glass and complete darkness, I could only hear the chirps of crickets and the pounding of my heart.

Hanging upside down in the flipped car, I tried to pull myself out onto the road. After a few minutes, I managed to slide out of the seat with only a few cuts on my skin from the shards of glass across the floor. No sign of Mandira.

Once I caught my ground, I stood up to see nothing but an endlessly empty road, surrounded by the dark trees of the woods. No sign of Mandira.

Hearing a buzzing sound that seemed to come from the glove compartment, I rushed to the other side of the car where

Mandira had been. I reached over and opened it to see if she had put her phone there which was maybe ringing. But I didn't find a phone. I found another gun. And a police badge with Mandira's identification on it. And a security two-way radio. That's where the buzzing was coming from.

A large streak of blood covered the ground right outside the shattered window of the passenger's seat...someone had dragged Mandira out of this car.

Following that path of blood, which abruptly disappeared a few feet away, I came across the tire streaks of another car across the tar. This crash was no accident. Mandira was gone...and now, she was in danger.

I crouched down and reached into the shattered window for the glove compartment. Grabbing the security radio, I turned the dial.

"Hello? Hello - is anyone there?" I asked urgently.

There was no response, just a continuous buzzing.

"If anyone can hear me, please I need your help. Mandira…someone's taken her. And she's in trouble - please, can anyone hear me," I asked again.

After a brief pause, I heard a click from the opposite side.

"Police. Could you repeat what you said? Your voice is breaking off," said the officer.

The officer's voice was sleep-deprived and groggy - as if he was woken up from a brief nap. He sounded like the stereotypical kind of officer in the movies who never cares about anything. You could hear the agitation in his voice.

"Mandira Bhatnagar - she's missing. Someone has taken her. She's in danger…please I need your help," I said into the radio.

"How long has she been missing?"

"I think it's been just over an hour. A jeep crashed into ours, and when I woke up, she was missing. I can see her blood on the pavement - she was dragged off," I said quickly. I could hear the worry growing in my voice.

"Calm down sir…you were in an accident? Sir…we can file a missing person's report only 24 hours after they have gone missing," said the officer sternly.

"She's a police officer in Mumbai - do you know her? Don't departments have files on officers? Mandira Bhatnagar. You have to help her - she's in danger," I begged.

"Sir, we don't have the Mumbai officers on file. We're a small department located 274 kilometers from Mumbai - your radio gets directed to the closest department. I don't know who Mandira is, but once 24 hours pass, you can file a report for her."

"I can't wait 24 hours damn it! She's in danger!" I shouted. "You have to help me! There was a man at the Chandni Cottages - he tried to rape her, and he raped two other young kids. I think he's the one who took her." There was no response. "Damn it! Are you even listening?" I yelled as I pounded my fist on the car in anger.

There was another momentary pause.

"Sir - 24 hours and you can call this station back."

And with that, he hung up. I stared at the radio for a few seconds, wondering why this area even had a police department.

There was only one thing I could do…it was the only option I had left to help Mandira. I had no phone. No other way to get in contact with anyone. I worried about her safety. Mine was not important. I dialed the radio one more time.

"Sir - you need t-"

"My name is Ahmed Kazemi," I said into the mic, cutting the officer off. "Someone has taken Mandira. She's in danger. Please...I need your help."

Chapter 9

I woke up and found myself lying on a cement floor with my hands chained to an old underground pipe. The scent of dry blood came upon me. I felt nauseous, light-headed, and exhausted. My vision was slowly starting to clear up and adjust to the dim light of the room. There wasn't much to see...nothing but a dirty mattress sitting at the opposite side of the room and a wall that hid the corner behind it.

I had no idea where I was...but I knew very well who had brought me here. Beyond the scent of my own blood was that blended scent of cologne and rum.

I tried to feel the touch of my phone, but it was gone. I was surrounded solely by silence and the droplets of pipe water that shattered as they hit the cold floor.

The silence was broken by the sound of a door opening from around the corner. At first, the sound of his footsteps clicking across the floor filled the silence of the room. Then, wearing his police uniform and a smirk of power across his face, Arman appeared from around the corner.

"You're a very beautiful woman Mandira. Very beautiful," he said as he licked his lips.

Immediately, images of Nima began to appear in my mind. Arman was a monster and the only thing that came with him wherever he went was destruction. There was this look of control in his eyes, as if he could and wanted to hurt me, just like he did to Nima. I was terrified...no matter how hard I tried in that moment, I could not rid myself of my fear of him.

He, with steps of confidence, walked closer, and as he quickly approached me, I slowly and pointlessly tried to move back, despite the chains wrapped tightly around my wrists. And the farther I stepped back, the tighter those chains became.

I wanted to look away, but at the same time, I couldn't take my eyes off him. He was the man that ended Nima's life so quickly and without hesitation. He was the man that proved to me how horrific human beings can become. How difficult it can be to bring justice to his victims.

I somehow managed to stand to my feet, almost collapsing as I reached an extent of balance. I took a few small steps back, disregarding the fact that there was truly nowhere else for me to go. As I stood, staring at Arman and slowly taking steps back, my back hit what felt like a massive brick wall and before I could see what it was, a brawny hand with piercing veins grabbed my arm tightly and forced me to turn around. A heavier sense of fear fell upon me - it was Arbazz, and this time, he looked much more aggressive and much more motivated to hurt me. It was the one and only time in my life that I have experienced such a fear that was so indescribable. I was paralyzed physically and mentally.

His grip was too strong - I couldn't get away from him. His eyes were bloodshot, and his breath reeked of alcohol. He was sweating heavily, but he was smiling as if he had finally won some kind of game. He pulled my body close to his and ran his fingers down my breasts. I tried to push away - nothing could be done.

Quickly, he forced me to face Arman, but he still pressed my body against his, with my back to his chest and one arm across my neck. He held his hand over my mouth tightly. I could feel his other hand reaching to unbutton my pants, his fingers treading inside. I went numb.

"Where's your Kabir, Mandira?" mocked Arman.

Arbazz began to chuckle crudely, tightening his hold on me and pressing his body into mine with greater force. I could feel his body attempting to cut into me. Only my muffled screams escaped his hands.

"Mandira, why would you risk your entire life for a terrorist like Kabir? It looks like those risks are paying off, huh," smirked Arman.

It was becoming harder for me to breathe. Arbazz was a big man, and his weight increasingly pressed down on my neck.

"Poor guy... he's handed himself over to the police with the hope of finding you. By the time they're done beating him, he won't even be able to utter his own name," laughed Arbazz.

"And Nima has probably been on your mind. I'm sorry beautiful...she needed to die - if she lived, it would have been me who would have died a much slower and painful death," grinned Arman as he looked to the floor and began to unbutton his shirt.

"She didn't want to listen to my threats Mandira...could you blame me for that?" he continued. "She tried to bring attention to my beautiful girls. Those kids make a ton of money for me. I provide them with food and some housing, and in return, they satisfy my customers who need that fantasy fulfilled," he grunted.

I held disgust in my eyes with each and every word he said. I had no idea he was running a trafficking ring.

"Oh, don't look so angry and disgusted," snapped Arman. "Mandira - it's business. That was the best way to get rid of any of the evidence that Nima could have presented against me - the photos, the testimonies, the underground money collection. Not to mention her rape test results, her doctors, her family...everything and everyone that could have testified for her was my problem...and I took care of that problem...almost," he said as he looked at me.

"Nima really loved you Mandira," said Arman. "I threatened your life when she tried to bring up my girls for the first time, so she kept you out of it to protect you. She tried to get rid of me on her own. Because without me as the boss...the provider for my babies, she knew my side business would crumble."

He brought his face closer to mine and spoke in a heavy whisper.

"There are just some things that need to be done, and when people don't want to help you in reaching your greatest potential...then it's time for you to crush theirs," he said as he pounded his fist on his other hand.

I struggled under Arbazz. The more I struggled, the further he pressed his fingers inside. I moaned in pain...it seemed like music to his ears.

"I can see the love you have for Kabir, Mandira. You slept with him, didn't you? Where did he touch you Mandira?

Here? How about here?" said Arman as he pressed his finger across my body. As Arbazz held on to me, he removed his hand to allow Arman to press his fingers to my lips and slowly tread his fingers down my body. Even with the opportunity to speak...to scream, I couldn't get myself to.

"Did he make you feel like a woman Mandira... the way I made Nima embrace her womanhood," smirked Arman. "Stop holding that look in your eyes my beautiful Mandira...what purpose do you think women serve? It's my job to show women how to feel like women."

His words cut through me like knives. I couldn't speak anymore. I couldn't breathe.

"It's too bad you know...I wish you hadn't given your virginity to Kabir...that belonged to me. I love the innocence, the purity, the pain that comes with a virgin. All my little girls started with me before they were placed in the business. But Nima…that woman was perfect. An insistent virgin that is no longer able to insist," laughed Arman. "But sometimes, a girl with some experience is good," he grinned as he moved the hair from my face.

He tightly held my face in his arms and pressed his lips against mine. I tried...I tried so hard to move away...to push him away, but I couldn't. He was a monster. I felt disgusted of my own body as both of them continued to touch me...I felt numb.

Arbazz held on to me and laughed as Arman stroked my face and moved his lips to my neck. His teethe began to sink into my shoulders - I felt as if my mind was slowly leaving my body - just to escape what was happening to me.

"Mandira - your body is so sweet. Your skin is so soft to the touch. Beautiful...I must say. Unfortunately, I made a promise - and you know me - I never break my promises," chuckled Arman.

He shifted his eyes to look at Arbazz.

"Arbazz - ready to taste her womanhood?" he asked playfully.

Suddenly, Arbazz lifted me and carried me forcefully to the mattress on the other side of the room. He was just too strong - every attempt I made to get away from him, he simply held down his grip more strongly. He threw me onto the bed and sat on top of me, his weight pushing me down further. I felt suffocated... trapped.

As Arbazz held me down, Arman came to the bedside and used his handcuffs to strap me to a metal pipe that hung slightly above the bed.

"Looking at you Mandira, I'm reminded of Nima. How beautiful she was. The look of desperation in her eyes, the strain at the nape of her neck - everything she did that evening to run away made me hold on to her more," he said as he tightened the cuffs. "Something about it just brings me pleasure. Scream Mandira. Moan for him Mandira. No one will be able to hear you. Enjoy this one Arbazz. Make her scream. Make her moan."

With that, Arman left the room, locking the door behind him.

Chapter 10

After Arbazz was done, he put his clothes back on and, while buttoning up his shirt, simply stared at me with a harsh grin on his face and pride in his stature. My body was in so much pain - he forced himself into me and had beaten me whenever I attempted to push him off. As a tear began to fall down my cheek, Arbazz bent over, wiped off my tear, and licked his fingers, almost as if he was enjoying the meat of a fresh kill. My hands were still tied to the bed. I had no energy left to be angry, to cry, or to even process what was happening.

Arbazz started saying things but I couldn't pay attention to him. I felt nauseous and my vision was blurred again. I felt lost. He had stopped forcing his body into mine, but that feeling of being overpowered and abused by him remained like a stain. Before I even realized it, Arbazz opened the last bottle of alcohol he had, and after taking one last sip, drenched it all over the bed and onto my body.

"Cheers beautiful!" he exclaimed with a vulgar grin.

He sat on top of me once again.

"So beautiful. The taste of your body...the flavor of your lips..."

He bent forward and licked my lips. His hands pressed against my stomach. I could taste the cheap scotch on his tongue. He moved his hands down my legs and gripped my ankles, forcing them to bend forward and encompass his heavy body. He kissed the nape of my neck. And raped me.

Again. And again. and again.

Chapter 11

Standing in the middle of the road, I could do nothing but wait. I paced back and forth, praying that the police would listen to me once they got here before they shot me. I needed to make sure that Mandira would be out of harm's way. I had no clue who had taken her, but I knew in my heart that she wasn't in good hands.

Soon, helicopters were hovering above me and the sirens of police jeeps were approaching. I held my hands in the air, clear to them all that I had no weapons on me and prayed that God would be on our side.

***

I woke up in a jail cell hanging by my wrists, wearing nothing but my black boxers. The last thing I remember was seeing some police jeeps coming down that long and empty road.

"I see you've gained consciousness...those sedation materials my officers use have different effects on everyone," said an officer in a highly decorated uniform. "Glad to see it only lasted a few days for you."

"A few days?" I thought to myself.

"Now it's time for you to give us information Mr. Kazemi. And if you don't...well...you're going to wish you never woke up," said the officer in a strict voice.

The officer rose his right hand as if he was calling someone forward. Before I could even take another breath, an officer came from behind and gave me three lashes on my back.

Just as he was about to give me a fourth lash, I yelled out in pain to the officer.

"I need your help sir," I said as I caught my breath.

"I can't help you if you can't help us," he shrugged. He signaled for the lashes to continue.

"Mandira Bhatnagar," I said out loud.

Suddenly, he held his hand up signaling the other officer to stay back. A look of confusion and surprise appeared on his face.

"What did you say?" he asked.

"Mandira Bhatnagar. She works with the police department - undercover agent. Sir, Mandira's in danger," I said.

"How do you know Mandira?" asked the officer as he stepped closer.

"Mandira found me on a roadside. I was on my way to death when she found me unconscious. She didn't know who I was. But she took me to the Chandni Cottages right outside of Mumbai. And she brought me back to good health. Please...please make sure that she is safe," I begged.

"Jagan - call Jamal," said the decorated officer.

The officer who had whipped my back nodded and left the room.

***

For about twenty minutes, we waited. The officer was continuously observing me as I hung with my hands tied to the low ceiling. Another officer was guarding the door. And another officer was cleaning the dirt from under his fingernails.

"My name is Kabir Malik sir. I'm not the terrorist you're looking for."

The officer looked down at the ground and laughed.

"You're the one who told us who you were. Changing your mind?" he mocked.

"Mandira was in danger sir. The police wouldn't have gotten to me as fast as they did that night if I didn't call in like that," I explained to him. "I know how the police are when it comes to missing persons reports. I want to make sure that Mandira is okay. Please tell me that she's okay sir," I pleaded.

He pulled open a drawer from the desk he was sitting on and took out a picture of me.

"Do you see this picture? Because I do," he said arrogantly. "So you and Ahmed must be twins. Right Sagar?" he said as he looked to another officer for sarcastic

218

confirmation. He crumpled the picture into a ball and threw it at my feet. He looked right into my eyes.

"You killed my wife in that explosion. She was a nurse on the third floor. I can't wait to see you die the slow and painful death you deserve."

Suddenly, he punched me hard in the stomach and knocked the air out of me for a moment. I bent forward trying to catch my breath, but my ropes kept me standing. And I couldn't blame the officer. I would have done the same thing.

As I was regaining my breath slowly, I saw Jamal walk into my cell accompanied by Jagan, the officer who had whipped me. Jamal was wearing his uniform, which held medallions representative of honor and bravery. I could see his sleeve tattoo, which I distinctly remembered from when I met him in Delhi. But his eyes were puffed up and red. And from that, I could tell that Mandira was not okay.

"These officers called to inform me that you have information about Mandira?" asked Jamal sternly.

I didn't think he recognized me. His tone was distant and unchanging. His voice was very coarse.

"Mandira has been with me for the last week Jamal. She found me on the side of the road more dead than I was alive and helped me get back up. We spent the last week together at the Chandni Cottages. And we found these young girls..." I tried to tell him. He seemed to ignore what I was saying. Not out of arrogance, but out of grief.

"You can refer to me as Officer Khan, Mr. Kazemi," he said coldly.

I tried to see if he could remember me. Maybe then he would be able to listen to what I was saying as truth.

"Do you remember me? I worked with you in Delhi a few months ago whe-"

"I remember you Kabir," he said as he looked me in the eyes. "But that doesn't change who you are now."

"So his name is Kabir?" asked an officer in disbelief.

"It doesn't matter," replied Jamal.

"Please, trust me. For the sake of Mandira," I said sincerely.

Jamal quickly grabbed me by my neck and looked at me with a mix of anger and sorrow.

"Do not put her name in your mouth. For the sake of Mandira? You raped my sister. You raped my sister," he broke into tears.

The surrounding officers stood back with as much surprise as I had listening to Jamal. It seemed like it was the first time Jamal had shared this information out loud.

"I would never hurt her Jamal. I would never hurt her Jamal. I love that girl. I would never hurt her...please tell me that she's with you Jamal. Please," I begged. My breathing was getting heavier. I wanted him to say that she was with him so badly. But in his grief, I saw loss. His tears told me that Mandira was gone.

"She's gone," he cried.

The officers surrounding us looked down to the floor, trying to respect the tears that came down Jamal's face. I felt tears coming from my own eyes, but my expression went blank. I would not believe that Mandira was gone. There was no way. I didn't want to believe it.

Jamal wiped his tears and tried to stop his grief, but I knew he couldn't. He loved Mandira. I could see that so clearly...he adored his sister. And felt pain in the reality that he couldn't protect her.

"A local villager had called the police after he saw a fire in the middle of the woods. By the time we got there, her body was burnt beyond my ability to recognize her. But after some DNA and blood tests, we identified that it was Mandira. The autopsy showed us that she had just recently been raped. And your DNA was found on her."

"Someone burned her body?" I asked in grief.

"She did it herself," he sorrowfully said as he stared at the wall behind me. "She hung herself in the middle of a fire that she created. The police reports show that she was the one who started the flames. She was feeling so broken when I last saw her...she must have felt so alone. She even tried to take her cremation into her own hands." Jamal's hands were on his head

as it looked like he was trying to process the reality he had

been told. But I felt that Mandira was alive. Even with

everything - the autopsy reports, the police investigation, and

her own brother's tears - I knew that Mandira was alive.

"There is no way she would take her own life Jamal," I

told him as I shook my head in disbelief. "She was planning

on it, I do know that, but she changed her mind. She was

feeling broken," I told him.

"She was feeling the burden of death on her own

shoulders, but she told me that she would never act on those

thoughts again Jamal. She didn't kill herself Jamal. I know in

my heart she didn't," I told him repeatedly.

"Mandira and I got to spend a lot of time together this

past week. I know that it was just a week but hear me when I

say this Jamal. I love Mandira. And I know that she loved me,"

I said truthfully. "Do you know why I say that? Because she

was willing to put her life on the line for me. She found out

about my face being published everywhere as the identified

terrorist. But she saw my truth. My life belongs to her. I'm not going to say I *loved* her because that would mean she was gone. I love that girl. I love her," I said sternly. "Help me find her Jamal."

He looked away from the wall and towards me, this time with less anger and more sorrow.

"I did her last rites yesterday Kabir. I did my little sister's final rites last night. Even if everything you're saying about your time with her was true, I can't take back what happened. Not even God can. Please don't push me to relive seeing my sister in sorrow Kabir," he said with a heavy breath. "Please," he said again.

He then pulled out a locket from his pocket and cradled it in his hands. It was Mandira's locket. A heart shaped locket from Zindagi that she never took off.

Except for when we were leaving the hospital.

Chapter 12

I don't even know how much time has passed since I'd been here. At least a few days. Arman had given me one of his bigger white shirts to wear since my original clothes had been completely torn after the first night with Arbazz. I had gashes across my body, bruises all over my skin. I could feel the bite marks on my neck and breasts and abdomen, which had slowly become infected. Two or three times a day, Arbazz and Arman, either together or separately, would come to ensure those marks remained. But the numbing pain in my mind was more than the numbing pain of my body.

My hands were still tied together with rope, but I wasn't chained to a pipe or wall anymore. There was no way for me to leave anyway. The walls of Arman's house were soundproof, and a key pad rested next to the basement door that locked me away from the rest of the world. Whenever they were finished with me for the time being, Arman or

Arbazz would punch in a few digits, hear a beeping sound, open the door, and be quick to close it behind them.

Some time back, perhaps a few nights ago, I saw the exact numbers Arman used to open the door. 3-6-6-1. After I knew he was gone for sure, I got up and punched those very numbers into that key pad. I thought that with the beeping sound, came freedom. But I then came to realize that there was a long staircase outside of that door that only led to another locked door with a different code. I banged on that door with my fists. Helplessly, I returned to that cold and cemented room.

When Arman got back from work that same day, he, with the help of Arbazz, tied me to the bed and placed a blindfold over my eyes. I remember listening to Arman laugh as Arbazz snapped one of my wrists. I found out that night that they had cameras watching me...that they knew I had tried to see their code for the door. And this was their way of punishing me. As I clenched my wrist in pain with my eyes covered and Arbazz still on top of me, the scent of my rose perfume surrounded me.

"I bought some of that perfume you always have on at work," grinned Arman. "It's nice on you."

I could feel the spray of perfume, and soon after, the warm breath of Arman on my neck. "It's very nice on you," he said as his teeth pressed into my skin.

***

The next day, I rested my broken wrist in the sink under the cold water in the bathroom of the basement, attempting to soothe the poignant and fresh pain. My first night here, I hadn't noticed the bathroom because it was hidden around a corner of the room that I could not reach with my chains, but it quickly became a place I tried to avoid. It was unkempt and had a putrid smell of sweat and feces. Only the light from the main room allowed me to see what was inside. The bathroom bulb had fused. There was a small box of pornographic magazines near the toilet, which was dirty and cracked. But it was the shower that I feared. I hadn't even bathed since my second night here.

I remember the second night I was here too vividly. Arbazz told me that I looked a bit dirty. He brought me Arman's white shirt and some black laced lingerie. He unlocked me from my chains and guided me to the bathroom. He nudged me into the shower and simply stared. There was no curtain to separate us. He stood and waited outside of the shower while I stood on that cold tile with the clothes he had given me, scared of what he expected from me. After a long pause, he laughed his vulgar laugh that I had become accustomed to.

"Aren't you going to take a shower?" he smirked.

I didn't respond. I didn't respond. But I knew he could sense the fear I had from my face. And he was testing my fear of him. He moved into the shower and turned the knob. I continued staring at the wall behind where he had originally stood. I could hear the water from the faucet pouring into a dirty bucket on the floor.

"Why so quiet tonight? Mandira...let me hear your voice."

I stayed silent. My mind was somewhere else...trying to help me hide from what I was expecting to happen.

He picked up a cup from the floor and used it to scoop some water out of the bucket. He took the clean clothes out of my hand and tossed them in the sink. Leaving the scraps of clothing I had on from the night that they had brought me here, he poured the water over my head.

"Consider this a baptism into your new life. Your own God cannot help you anymore my dear Mandira. But I can. Stay obedient and you will come to love this new life of yours," he mockingly whispered.

I continued to stare at the wall. His words told me that they weren't planning on killing me anytime soon. But I could see death on the horizon. Not physically. But my death was on the horizon.

"I think this was Rhea's favorite part," said Arbazz, breaking the silence. "Kids love playing in the water. I remember her standing in my shower with Meera. Rhea was a nice surprise. I was just looking to have a little fun with Meera - all I did was pretend to be a teacher from Meera's school to get Madhu away from her. Then, I told Meera that her brother had met with an accident and needed her. Meera dropped everything and rushed over to see her brother, except for Rhea. Rhea was the one thing Meera could not drop. Meera was teaching her how to read when she got my call. Poor girl didn't know that I was going to teach them both a few things too," he grinned.

My heart ached thinking about Meera and Rhea. Meera must have felt like it was her fault that Rhea fell into Arbazz's hands. Both of them could have never known. And after all that Arbazz had done to those girls, I felt like Meera saw that the blame for Rhea's death fell upon her. I prayed in my heart that Meera could find peace in her pain. None of it was her fault.

"I will let you clean yourself up this time. But next time, I'll be sure to join you. Meera and Rhea showed me that it can be a lot of fun," he grunted. "I'm going to take up what Arman is doing and not try to break my promise to you either."

He stepped out, walked back into the main room, and closed the bathroom door behind him.

***

One evening, I was lightly asleep on the floor with my hands chained loosely to the ground with some nails. My body was sore. I was bruised and bleeding. The coolness of the floor was my only comfort as it slightly soothed the aches in my back. I could hear the basement door open and close briefly, and soon, the sound of someone's steps coming closer grew. I didn't even have enough energy to open my eyes.

I suspected that it was just Arman or Arbazz coming back to get today's share. But this time, I was gently shaken awake and in a concerned whisper, I could hear my name. Immediately, I recognized the voice.

"Jagan?" I said as I turned to see him crouching beside me with worry across his face.

"Mandira," he whispered. He gently stroked the cuts across my shoulder.

"Jagan?" I said a bit louder. "How did you find me?"

"What have they done to you?" I could hear shock and confusion in the tone of his voice.

"We need to get out of here - they'll be back soon," I said quickly. "Can you get me out of these chains?"

Jagan reached forward and began to tug at the chain that was clasped around my wrists, but after a few tugs, he sat back, resting himself on his knees. He put his hands through his hair in a way that looked frustrated.

"Let me try something else," he said calmly.

Slowly, he held me by my side and sat on top of me. As his expression shifted towards laughter, mine transitioned into shock. He leaned forward and with his hand pressed gently against my stomach, began to kiss me. I backed my head away from him and pulled at the chains that held me down.

"It's okay Mandira - I'm not engaged anymore." He leaned in closer, holding my neck as he pressed his lips against mine. As quickly as I could, I pulled at my chain sharply and punched Jagan in the cheek. As the chain pinched the skin on my wrists, I pulled my hands back to the ground while Jagan sat up, looked to the side, and felt his jaw.

I was breathing heavily, trying to understand what was happening. As Jagan held one hand to his jaw, he quickly slapped me across my face, forcing me to turn my cheek against the floor. He grabbed my neck and lightly placed his lips on my other cheek.

"Nima said you would be aggressive," he laughed. "But I told her that I would be too."

"You helped kill Nima?" I asked in shock. "How could I have not seen that?" I said with a deep breath.

"She didn't see it coming either Mandira. And it wasn't just me. It was Arman. Arbazz. His brother, Ramesh," he said as he counted them on his fingers.

"Why would you do that to her? She loved you," I said in disbelief.

"And I loved her too. Nima was very strict on waiting until marriage. And I respected that. But being who I am, I couldn't wait. I needed it," he groaned. "So much that it kept on tapping into my thoughts, but I tried to hide that from Nima and well, from everyone. But Arman understood where I was coming from. He could see and understand that continuous hunger in my thoughts," said Jagan as he traced the cut on my cheek with his finger. "So he convinced me to try out his business and introduced me to Parthavi, a beautiful and innocent sixteen-year-old girl he had bought from a trade in Bengal. And like that, my hunger went away. Enough for me to wait until the wedding. And everything was fine. I was ready to get married. I loved Nima…I really did," he said coarsely. "But she was too focused on Arman towards the end. She found out about his business and found a way to access everyone who had paid for some services through a mole in his business," he said shaking his head. "And she was ready to release that information to the press as soon as she got it. But before she saw my name on there, I gently took the book she had with all the exchanges, names, and payments and told her to calm down and think rationally, especially about how dangerously Arman would act towards her once she released that information. And I hoped that she would just let it go. But she didn't want to listen," he said as he clenched his teeth in anger. "She grabbed a phone and started to dial the number of one of her friends who was a reporter, so I stopped the call and told her that we, together, could stop Arman. That I couldn't risk losing her. I told her I could get him by himself. And, as I expected, she trusted me. So I arranged it with the help of Arman. And Arbazz. And Ramesh. "

"You took her to that building..." I was still so surprised.

"I can still see her trying to shoot at him as he stood right in front of her," laughed Jagan. "But no bullets flew. I had already taken them out and handed them to Arman, who took her bullets out of his own pocket and dropped them on the floor," he said, mimicking that moment. "And then, I grabbed her from behind. I could feel her world freeze as she recognized what was happening. But we couldn't kill her just yet. Many years ago, when my father was participating in the revolution back home, they couldn't execute women who were virgins. So we each took our own turn with her. And as Ramesh held her down for me, Nima maliciously warned me that Allah would give me what I deserved. And that you would find her justice. I pressed a knife into her stomach as she said those words," he grunted.

"You killed an innocent girl!" I yelled furiously. "She was so in love with you! And I thought you were in love with her too…how could you have done that?" I said as my voice traced off in shock.

"There was nothing else I could do. She would've found out that I was on that list and would've left me anyway. Maybe even killed me. And even if she didn't, I was looking at a lifetime in prison if that list got out. I remember talking to her one last time in the hospital before we detonated those bombs. She kept on repeating your name slowly. She couldn't recognize me or say my name. But there was fear in her eyes -

like a subconscious memory. I had done my job well," he smiled. "But Mandira - that's the past. Don't concern yourself with that," he said as he tapped my cheek.

As he bent forward and bit my neck, I quickly pulled out one of the nails that had held my chains down and stabbed it into the side of his neck, directly into his jugular vein.

Once Jagan had positioned himself on top of me, I had realized that his initial few tugs on my chains had lifted out one of the nails from the ground. I began trying to untwist the remaining portion from the floor as he prided himself for Nima's death. And once Jagan's neck was in reach, I sharply pulled my hand from the floor as the cuffs pinched my skin to get the nail where it needed to go.

Jagan clasped at his neck and tried to remove the nail. But the more he pulled at it, the quicker he lost blood. He got up but immediately fell to his knees beside me, gasping for air. He collapsed and reached his hand towards me and then back at his neck.

I sat in the corner of that basement, thinking to myself as Jagan bled out in front of me. Thinking about Nima. Thinking about ending my own life right then and right there. But I couldn't get myself to do it. It would have been easier. And all I needed was Arman's razor blade in the bathroom. But I couldn't do it. I had just a bit of hope that I couldn't get myself to let go of. The hope that someone would find me. My faith rested on Jamal, Simran, and Kabir.

***

About a half an hour later, Arman came into the room, immediately seeing Jagan, dead and surrounded in blood.

"I told him you're a smart girl," he chuckled, as he felt his beard. He walked over, and pulling Jagan by the arms, dragged his body across the floor and behind the corner wall. "Arbazz can deal with the rest," he grunted, wiping his hands on his shirt.

"Surprised?" he asked sarcastically.

"I had no idea," I said shaking my head again in disbelief.

"Jagan was a good one, especially after Ahmed gave Nima my list," he said casually.

"Ahmed?" I asked wondering if he was referring to Kabir.

"I forgot you don't have all the details of what happened," he said as he looked up at me. "Ahmed worked for me. A nineteen-year-old kid. Helped me kidnap many of the girls for my business, until suddenly he seemed to be hit by an angel and decided to give information to Nima that could end my business and give me the death penalty."

"Ahmed Kazemi?" I asked as I connected the information.

"That's the real one," laughed Arman. "After everything I had done for that kid after saving him from living on the streets," he shook his head in disgust. "As soon as I told Jagan that it was Ahmed that was responsible for the list leak, he helped me burn that boy alive."

And then it clicked. The name Ahmed Kazemi seemed so familiar to me because I had seen his name written on a patient chart when I had been working in the burn unit of the hospital a few days before the explosion.

"Kazemi was unrecognizable after we took care of him," smirked Arman. "And he had no written records outside the hospital…no living relatives. It was a perfect name to give the blame for the attack and link it to Kabir's picture."

"Why Kabir?" I asked as things were now starting to make sense.

"Wow - Arbazz did a great job of beating Kabir if he couldn't remember enough to tell you," said Arman as he shook his head in approval. "Kabir must have heard us being a bit loud with Nima in that building," he laughed. "While Ramesh was being intimate with Nima, Kabir came from behind and stabbed Ram. Ram quickly got off Nima and tried to hit Kabir, but before he could, Kabir slit Ram's throat. It was brutal Mandira," he said as he stared out at a distance. "Kabir is a strong man. Nima thought he could save her, and he wanted to. He tried so hard to help her. But Arbazz, Jagan, and myself were able to knock him unconscious after a bit of a struggle. Kabir became especially weak after Jagan injected him with some leftover drug he had used on Nima to calm her down," he grinned. "Arbazz said he could take care of getting rid of Kabir and wanted the opportunity to avenge his brother's murder at the hands of your lover," grunted Arman. He removed his watch and dropped it on the floor.

"Everything was set. Arbazz got rid of Kabir with the help of one of my other men, while Jagan and I executed the attack here. We even got a college kid to wear a bomber jacket by threatening to pull his two younger sisters into our business after he failed to deliver his payment for a previous girl he had bought. Everything was set, until our Mandira decided to take a drive and coincidentally run into Kabir, who should have rotted in those woods," said Arman as he grabbed me by my hair. "You know, Arbazz called me, telling me that a woman had found Kabir and was staying at his property to take care of him. I had no idea it was you. I told him to finish off Kabir and bring 'that woman' along for us to celebrate a little. But that fool waited, telling me that he had a couple of other girls he was managing at the moment," he sighed. "And a few days into your stay, he said that the woman's name was Mandira, and I realized exactly who she was," said Arman as he moved the hair from my face. "But everything's alright now. Everything is going to be okay Mandira," he said sadistically.

***

Arman was sitting on the mattress, fiddling with some pills. He had been forcing me to take homemade pills. He said that condoms took away the pleasure of being inside of me but emphasized that he couldn't have me pregnant just yet. I told him that I just needed some birth control, but he firmly believed that those kinds of pills wouldn't stop me from getting pregnant. The pills he gave me induced me to vomit and continued to make me feel nauseous for hours after I had taken them. He had just given me a pill this morning. I had already vomited four times within the hour that I was given that pill. After that, all I could vomit was my own saliva.

The pills made me dizzy and gave me some of the worst headaches I've ever experienced in my life. And I had lost a lot of weight. The veins in my hands became especially prominent. I sometimes felt like I had been going in and out of consciousness. I was no longer sure how long I had been in this basement.

"Mandira, does this look familiar to you?" asked Arman sarcastically.

Arman reached into his pocket and grabbed a necklace that he held with pride. It was my necklace... I had given it to Meera the night Kabir and I left the hospital. But the locket was gone.

"Surprised? It just seems that everyone you try to help only ends up in a worse situation. First Kabir, now Meera," he smirked.

"What did you do to her Arman? Don't you dare hurt her Arman...don't you dare," I said as I pulled at my chains with the instinct to choke him.

"We took care of her...we did for her what she was going to do for herself anyway. And good news - she served an actual purpose because of us."

245

He threw several photographs down in front of me. At first, it was hard to see, but I soon realized that these were investigative photos. And as I realized what I was seeing, I began to breathe heavily and cry hysterically.

"Now tell me Mandira...what do you see?" he asked mockingly.

"You did this...how could you do this...she was a human being...she was a child...why would you do this...wh..." I broke off into tears.

"Relax Mandira...she was already dead when we found her. Poor girl...hung herself in a tree. I think she could have died a little less painlessly and shamefully, don't you think Arbazz."

Arbazz, who had just entered the room, chuckled...I wished those pills could make me deaf to keep me from hearing him.

"You did this to her...you took her…"

"I said relax Mandira...I know it's hard for you to see," shrugged Arman. "But tell me, who do you see? I see a burned body...a body so burned and charred that no one can tell who she is."

"Meera...Meera, I'm sorry Meera," I said out loud. I couldn't stop my hysteria. My tied hands dragged across the pictures in agony and remorse.

"To you and me, this is Meera. But to the world, this is Mandira," Arman said confidently.

Arman knelt down and pulled my face towards him, with his hands holding my head up and away from the pictures of Meera. He admired my agony.

"Meera was gone already...but the real question for everyone is, 'Where's Mandira?'"

"What?" I asked him as I felt my own tears.

"Where's Mandira? She's right here in this picture. She's the one that was found dead...found burned in the middle of the woods. That's exactly what the police believe. Meera doesn't exist to them...and Mandira no longer exists to them."

"You used Meera to convince the police that I was dead?"

"The police, your brother, Kabir...everyone. You would be surprised to see how easy it can be for me to falsify evidence, investigative reports, an autopsy," he said arrogantly. "I know you've wondered how I've been able to get rid of all the complaints and cases against me. Well, I have access to all the information. And with just a few clicks of a button or a few calls, everything and anything can be turned in my favor," he snickered. "You should have seen your brother as he looked at your pyre. He really loved you. And poor Kabir - my scapegoat. He really really loved you. I gave him a visit a few days ago…and a very good beating for all of his horrible horrible actions," smirked Arman again. "You know what I told him - I told him that he had no right to touch you as I punched him in the stomach six times - one for every night you spent together at those cottages. Knocked the air out of him. And, personally, it was more fun watching your brother take out his pain on Kabir," he laughed as he bent down to one knee and held his hand over my ear, passing his fingers through my hair.

"This will always be our little secret. Now take your clothes off Mandira...I'm feeling a little hungry," he said, loosening his shirt.

"Get the hell away from me," I said in disgust.

"Mandira...I know this is a tougher pill to swallow...Meera was probably a sweet girl. And I'll make sure that Kabir gets the death penalty for that explosion - he won't be in pain for much longer," he whispered as he stroked through my hair. "Let me make you feel a little better Mandira. Take your clothes off," he demanded.

I got up and stepped away from him. There was nowhere to run...nowhere to go...but I needed somewhere else to be.

"Now that Meera's gone, you wouldn't want anything to happen to Madhu, now would you?"

"Madhu..."

"Arbazz!" shouted Arman.

Suddenly, from the other corner of the room, I saw Madhu get thrown to the ground with Arbazz standing right behind. Madhu was handcuffed from the back, bleeding from his forehead, and beaten badly.

"Don't touch him...please...he's just a kid. Leave him alone!" I begged.

"Take your clothes off Mandira," repeated Arman.

"Don't listen to him Mand-" yelled Madhu. But before he could finish speaking, Arbazz pulled out a knife and swiftly stabbed Madhu in the stomach.

"Madhu!" I cried out loud.

Arman held me back from running to Madhu's side.

"I will do whatever you want me to do...please just let him go," I said, turning to face Arman.

"Hold the knife Arbazz," said Arman, holding his hand up to tell Arbazz to wait. "Mandira, I've tasted your body...but not completely. I want to feel like I'm your husband. I want you to undress me, touch me, kiss me, make love to me...just the way you do it for Kabir," he said as he leaned forward and kissed my cheek. "Take off your clothes Mandira," he whispered again into my ear.

"He needs to get to a hospital...he needs to see a doctor," I said softly behind my tears.

"You are his doctor Mandira. For every ten minutes you spend with me, I will give you five minutes with him. I promise. You were able to keep Kabir alive...I'm sure you can do the same for Madhu. I won't say it again. Take off your clothes Mandira," repeated Arman again.

I listened. I unbuttoned my shirt and was left standing in nothing but the black lace lingerie I had been forced to wear in front of Arman. Arman, who was wearing his police uniform, simply stood before me, gawking like the twisted man that he was.

I walked towards Arman and ran my hand down his chest. I wish I had a knife running down his chest instead. I could feel his badges...badges that stood for honor, sacrifice, and bravery. I couldn't help but rip them off as I unbuttoned his shirt.

"A little aggressive huh," he grinned.

I couldn't help but think...I had joined this crime branch with the hope of making a difference in the lives of others. I didn't have any medallions, but I still held great confidence and pride in the uniform that I wore...that he wore. But that was all gone...that image of justice and positive change. As I pulled at his medallions, my frustration became blinding.

As I pulled his shirt off his shoulders, he quickly pressed my body against the wall. For a moment, he stared at me fiercely with his heavy breathing while I stared down at the ground.

"Continue my love," he said with an attitude of control.

I reached down at his belt and loosened the buckle. He pressed his lips down into my neck and shoulders, and as he began to press me harder against the wall, my eyes locked on to Madhu, who was in a pool of blood at the other side of the room. He was breathing...but I knew that time was ticking. His eyes were shut, and his mouth was dry...his head was beaten, his chest swollen. Ten minutes with Arman seemed like an eternity...but all I needed were those five minutes with Madhu.

"Keep going Mandira...come on and love me Mandira," moaned Arman.

I pressed my lips against his and continued kissing him for as long as he would allow me to. I was trying to move slowly...trying to make the ten minutes without going too far. His hand moved slowly up my back. Soon, he was unhooking my bra and pressing my body closer to his. He forced me to the floor, and slowly, he managed to lay on top of me.

"This is what I've been looking for...both of us are relaxed...no force...no rape...just love," he groaned as Arbazz watched. Arman grabbed the blanket from the bed and rested the sheet just over my breasts. Just as his fingers were reaching to take my last piece of clothing off, his timer went off.

I pushed him off me, and quickly grabbed the shirt I had been wearing. He made no attempt to keep me down.

"As I always say, I never break my promises," sighed Arman.

As I was rushing towards Madhu, I loosely put my shirt back on and grabbed the shirt of Arman's uniform that had been lying on the floor next to his pants and belt.

I knelt down beside Madhu and immediately applied pressure to his stab wound, which went in quite deep. My hope was that none of his organs had been torn open. I felt his pulse...faster and faster it went each moment. I ripped a part of Arman's uniform and wrapped it tightly around Madhu's wound to help add pressure and stop some of the bleeding.

"Good thing I took these next few days off to spend some true quality time with you Mandira - I would have gotten into trouble if I didn't have my uniform," laughed Arman.

He knew he would never get into trouble - he always had enough connections to get out of even the slightest hint of trouble.

The stab wound on Madhu was just like the ones that covered Kabir's body the night I found him as well as Nima's. There was no doubt in my mind that the same knife was used on the three of them.

Slightly, Madhu's eyes began to open.

"Madhu, stay with me Madhu," I said to him.

"Di...don't...worr…" he said, struggling to speak.

"Please don't leave me Madhu...please," I said to him as his eyes began to close.

"Time's up...my turn," said Arman from behind me.

I held on to Madhu's hand, trying to keep track of his pulse to see if there were any changes. As I ran my fingers across his forehead trying to see how hard he had been beaten, Arman pulled me away from Madhu and threw me on the ground. Madhu's blood now covered Arman's hands.

"I'm a very fair man Mandira...don't break my rules."

Just as he was getting ready to sit on top of me again, we both heard a voice from upstairs.

"Mandira! Mandira!"

I could feel Arman's sudden tension in his grip around my wrists. It was Jamal.

As soon as we heard Jamal's voice, Arbazz was quick to come over and place his hand over my mouth.

"Mandira!" shouted Jamal again.

"How did your brother get in my house!" asked Arman in a threatening whisper.

I tried to move myself away from their grips, but Arbazz put all his weight into his hand to prevent me from screaming out to Jamal while Arman's grip was only getting tighter on my wrists.

"Mandira! Are you here?" yelled Jamal.

Arman leaned in towards me, with Arbazz's hand still covering my mouth.

"Jamal..." Arman mockingly whispered into my ear. "She's downstairs in the basement Jamal. Your sister is beautiful. So beautiful that I was thinking of getting her pregnant soon," he said as he traced his fingers down my stomach.

I could hear Jamal calling out my name upstairs. He was so close...his voice as close as Arman's lips were to mine. I yelled for Jamal, but nothing except for my muffled agony could be heard under Arbazz's hand.

"Don't you say a word! Don't you make one sound!" whispered Arman aggressively into my ear. "I will kill Madhu before you can get Jamal's attention Mandira...and I will kill Jamal if you dare try to let him know you're here," he said, shaking my wrists with a tightening grip.

Arman suddenly dug his other hand under the mattress next to us and frantically began searching for something. Within moments, he pulled out some cloth, tape, and climbing rope. He quickly shifted his hand from my wrists to my throat, forcing my breathing to stop. As I clenched at my neck, trying to grasp for air while also attempting to push away his tight grip, he scrunched up the cloth and pushed it into my mouth.

With one hand still at my throat, he bit off a large piece of tape and pressed it over my lips. Finally, he let go of my neck, but Arbazz moved over and held me down by my chest. Arman quickly worked to tie me to a pipe that rested just above the bed and on the wall. I could do nothing to stop him...simply trying to gain my breath back was like trying to breathe under water.

After restraining me as much as they could, Arman got up quickly and headed towards the door. I looked at him with disgust and hatred, but at the same time, I was begging for him to not hurt Jamal or Madhu.

"I'll be back soon...don't try anything stupid Mandira. I'm just going to convince him that he has to move on...I have no intention of hurting your brother...don't make me change my mind Mandira," he said, shaking his finger at me. "Arbazz...do whatever you need to make sure that the both of them stay quiet."

With that, Arman entered the key code, opened the door, and left.

Chapter 13

I found myself in Arman's living room, shouting for Mandira, hoping that she would respond. Dusty, cold, and dark, the room smelled of a heavy cologne.

Fingerprints, bomb structures, hospital floor plans… everything in the investigation traced back to Kabir. I even took my anger out on him. During his interrogation, I beat him badly. All I could think about was the pain someone was capable of inducing on my sister. The devastation that someone was capable of committing to so many innocent lives in that hospital. And in the height of my emotion, Kabir was that someone. But I felt that I made a mistake - a horrible mistake.

As I beat Kabir, he didn't fight back - he didn't get angry. He just asked for a listening ear. It was almost as if he was wanting for me to get rid of all of my pain on him just so I could listen to him. And it worked.

With every passing day, I had slept less and less as I believed Kabir more and more. My hope of ever seeing Mandira again diminished with the flames of her pyre, but the way Kabir spoke of Mandira…there was truth in his voice. And I wanted to believe him. I could hear Mandira in his truth. And I would never rest knowing that there was even the slightest chance that Mandira was still in harm's way.

Kabir told me about how Mandira spoke about her life in Uttar Pradesh and her experience with Ayan - intimate and brutal details that she never told anyone but me, Sim, or Zindagi. A part of me wondered if I was being fooled by Kabir - that he had somehow manipulated my sister. But Mandira's an intelligent woman - there was no way she could be manipulated by a stranger's charm.

Kabir shared information about their stay at a cottage outside of town and about an encounter with two young girls and a violent cottage owner. Mandira never once mentioned anything aside from the name of that cottage property in our most recent calls since the hospital explosion, but Kabir's stories of Mandira mirrored my expectations of Mandira. His concern for her ran deep - I could see the desperateness for Mandira's safety in his eyes. He loved Mandira, and despite all the pressing evidence against him, all I wanted to do was believe in his truth. And with a single phone call, I did.

I received a call in the middle of the night that Kabir was being restless and shouting at officers to bring me in again - no one initially listened, but a few days later, my friend Aamir called me and told me that I should check out what was going on with Kabir.

Immediately, I headed to the prison and told all the guards to remove themselves from Kabir's cell before I entered. I needed to speak with him...listen to him by myself.

Stepping inside, I found Kabir beaten brutally, with blood coming through his teeth and his right eye blackened. I came towards him and unlocked him from his restraints. He fell to his knees immediately.

"It's that officer - the one with his shirt buttons lose. The one with the scratches on his neck. I can smell Mandira's

263

perfume on him. It's light, but it's there Jamal. Underneath that heavy cologne, I can smell her. Those scratches behind his neck must have come from her. It's him," he said with conviction as he struggled to breathe. As I tried to help Kabir up, he gently pushed my hand away. "I'll catch up - protect Mandira from that monster."

Mandira's words began to ring in my ears - words I had forgotten in my anger and sorrow.

"Monsters are real…and still, no one can see them…how many women does it take for people to see Arman?"

I stood calling out to Mandira in Arman's living room, hoping I wasn't too late.

***

I was struggling under Arbazz. He was pressing down on my abdomen and holding me down by my neck. I was already restrained enough to where he didn't need to hold me down. But he took so much pleasure in his power over me. If I could just find a way to let Jamal know that I was here...

"Jamal! Help! Mandira is here! Jamal!" yelled Madhu as loud as he could.

He was putting himself at the face of death. Arbazz quickly got up and picked up his knife that he had thrown to the ground in his rush to hold me down when Jamal had come inside. I screamed at Arbazz to not hurt Madhu, but it meant nothing. The tape on my mouth hindered my screams, and Arbazz would never listen to me.

Arbazz turned Madhu to face him and stabbed him three times in the stomach. No hesitance. Madhu screamed in pain. I pulled at my ropes, but they would not loosen. I screamed in desperation. Arbazz lifted Madhu by his collar and smirked at Madhu's paleness.

"Looks like our chef wants to become a hero," laughed Arbazz.

Just as Arbazz was going to stab Madhu again, the sound of a gunshot and glass shattering came from above, followed by silence. Arbazz dropped Madhu and paused for a second. We both were waiting to see that the person we were dependent on would say something. But the silence continued. Arbazz came over to me to check on the ropes around my hands and then went towards the basement door. He entered the code and closed the door behind him.

I needed to get to Madhu somehow. I was lying on the floor next to that dirty mattress. Remembering how Arman had just pulled rope and tape from underneath, I hoped that I could find something that I could use to cut me loose from my ropes.

I turned my body as much as I could and tried to pull the mattress closer to my hands by grasping the bed with my feet. Once the mattress was within reach, I pulled it closer, trying to pull it in a way that allowed me to drag the contents underneath it along with the bed. I stretched my fingers outward and tried frantically to find something.

At first, I found only the handle of a knife and no blade. Hoping that each part had just separated, I continued feeling across the floor beneath the mattress, and within a few seconds, found the blade. I quickly pulled it out and began to cut through each of the ropes on my arms. When I felt the ropes loosen suddenly, I stretched my hands in opposite directions

and heard the last knot snap. I dropped the blade and ran

towards Madhu.

Chapter 14

"Jamal?" Arman called out as he came around the corner. "What are you doing in my house?"

"Where's Mandira?" I asked abruptly as I stared at Arman.

"Jamal? Is everything alright?" said Arman, attempting to sound sincere. "Mandira was killed - her body was found...you know that."

I pulled out my gun and pointed it directly at him. I could smell Mandira's perfume on him.

"Where's Mandira?" I asked again.

Arman held his hands in the air.

"Whoa...wait. Jamal relax...put your gun down Jamal. Let's talk about this...Mandira isn't here. You cremated her yourself just a few days ago," he said with conviction.

"Jamal! Help! Mandira is here! Jamal!" I heard as my ear turned towards the floor beneath me. The voice was faintly audible. It was desperate and sounded like it was coming from a young boy. There was a momentary silence between Arbazz and I as we repeated that voice in our heads again.

"Well isn't that just unfortunate," said Arman. He quickly pulled out a gun and aimed it at me.

Immediately, I shot him in the knee. He collapsed to the ground, knocking off a large glass vase from the bookshelf and dropping his gun as his bullet shot through the floor. I ran towards him and grabbed him by his collar, pressing him against the floor. I could see the scratches on his neck. I could smell Mandira's perfume.

"What did you do to her?"

"I made her feel like a woman," he said with an arrogant smile.

I lifted him by his collar and smashed him against the ground. My grip around his neck became tighter.

"I know you're upset. You're a cop and you couldn't even protect your sister."

I started to choke him. I could feel his pulse and the scratches Mandira had put on his neck.

"Your pain. My victory," he gasped.

Just as Arman's eyes began to close, I felt a sudden shock to my lower back. As I looked down, I saw blood coming through my shirt. Before I could turn around, I felt a club to my head. I collapsed to the ground beside Arman. My vision became blurry and my ears began to ring.

***

I pressed my hands against Madhu's stomach. I could feel his breathing get slower and slower.

"Didi..." said Madhu in a strained voice.

"Madhu - I'm so sorry Madhu," I said to him as I put additional pressure on his cuts.

"Don't worry about me. I'm a warrior," he said as he gently pounded his chest.

His hands then grasped at his stomach, and he winced in pain. Madhu began to fade in and out of consciousness.

"Madhu - stay with me yaar. Keep your eyes open Madhu."

I began searching the room for something…anything that could help Madhu.

And then I saw an opportunity.

Arbazz's hands were covered in blood and after he punched in the numbers on that key pad, the digits 3, 6, and 1 were the only buttons that held that blood. The passcode consisted of some new four-digit combination of those numbers, and I had to figure it out. It was the only opportunity available...and it needed to work. Madhu would die in this basement otherwise.

***

As I began to regain consciousness, I could see Arman standing above me with a club clenched in his hand. Another man stood beside me, pressing the barrel of a gun against my temple. The stench of alcohol filled the room.

"You don't know her like I do," Arman said with a grin. "You don't love her like I do."

"Please - just let her go. Stop hurting her Arman!"

"Hurting her?" he said sarcastically. "She's satisfying my needs and I'd like to think that I'm satisfying hers," he said as he crouched down beside me. "To be honest, in the beginning it was tough...tough to control her, so we did hurt her," he said pointing to himself and the other man. "But after a few punishments, her body adjusted to ours. She's understood that she belongs to us...that we control her," he smirked as he clenched his fists.

I struggled to get up. I wanted to kill him...beat him to death with my own hands. But I could not even stand up. I could feel the crack in my skull as my blood dripped down my face.

"I don't think we've formally met," laughed the other man beside me. "I'm Arbazz - your sister's other source of pleasure." Arman chuckled as he listened. "You know Jamal, I usually don't like taking on responsibility, but being in control of a woman like that...I'm proud I was born into this life as a man. I made sure that she knew that," coarsely whispered Arbazz.

Suddenly, I had the strength to get up. I had to. For Mandira.

I quickly got up, grabbing the gun and shooting the man who had been standing beside me directly in the heart. But before I could turn to shoot Arman, he shot me in the wrist, forcing me to drop my gun. Arman then shot me in the chest twice as he ran towards me and pointed the gun towards my forehead. I collapsed to the ground.

"Mandira is stronger than you," I told Arman as I clenched my chest. "You can put this bullet through my head. She's 100% worth that sacrifice. But you will not finish Mandira. She will finish you," I assured him.

"I'll let a piece of her finish you off first."

He reached behind him, pulling out Mandira's gun from underneath his belt. He tucked his own gun behind him, replacing where Mandira's gun had been resting.

"I pulled this gun out of Mandira's belt. She'll be devastated to hear that you died from her own bullet," said Arman as he took a close look at the gun. "Any last words you would like me to share with your sister."

"Nothing I need to tell you. She already knows."

Mandira knew that I loved her with all my being. And I had faith that she would be the one to stop Arman. I didn't have enough strength to defend myself. I couldn't even get up to reach my gun which rested on the floor behind Arman.

"The one thing I've noticed is that you aren't begging for your life. That's the one thing Mandira would beg for. She wouldn't beg for her own life. But she would beg to protect you. She would beg to protect Kabir. Now she's downstairs begging for the life of a kid she met just a couple of weeks ago. And I love it when she begs," he laughed cruelly.

Closing my eyes, I heard the click of the gun as Arman adjusted the barrel.

"Beg," said another voice.

I opened my eyes to see Mandira standing behind Arman with my gun pointed at his head. Her clothes were torn, and bruises, cuts, and bite marks covered her body. Fresh blood was dripping off her hands and down her arms. In her eyes, there was sorrow and rage. But I also saw strength. And determination.

Arman, keeping the gun pointed at my forehead, looked to the side and began to laugh out loud. He shook his head mockingly in disappointment.

"My dear Mandira, you should know better than to interrupt me when I have a gun pointed at your brother. I didn't want you to have to watch your brother die, but I'll be here to comfort you in my own way afterwards." He turned his head slightly towards her. "And I would never beg to a woman. It's my job to teach you to be submissive to me, and I'll make sure you know that before the sun comes out."

Arman quickly lifted the gun, and pointing it at me, pulled the trigger. I winced at the click of the gun, but there was no bullet fired. With a confused and frustrated look on his face, Arman pulled the trigger once more, but again, there was no resulting shot. He opened up the cylinder and shook it, causing seven bullets to fall to the ground. It was fully loaded.

"You're using my gun," said Mandira. "A gun that I built so that no one else could shoot it besides me."

Arman turned away from me and looked at Mandira. The confusion on his face quickly turned into fear. As he focused on her, I grabbed the gun that was tucked at his belt. Mandira kept her eyes locked on Arman and tightly gripped the gun in her hand. But as she kept her eyes locked on Arman, the perimeter of Arman's house was quickly surrounded with police officers.

Soon, they had broken down the front door and were filed in the room, covered in protective gear from head to toe. But their guns weren't pointed at Arman...they were pointed at Mandira.

"Mandira - put your gun down Mandira!" yelled one of the officers. "Put the gun down Mandira. If you shoot him, you will be arrested. We can talk about this Mandira - this is not the way to deal with this situation," said another head officer.

Mandira ignored their instruction. Not once did she stop looking at Arman.

"Just before the hospital explosion, Nima had become slightly conscious," she said directly to Arman. "And in the few moments I had left with her, she told me that you would be coming for me next. That you promised to kill me and those I love with my own gun. That you whispered that to her again and again as you raped her. Those words were the only ones she could repeat over and over again."

I could see tears streaming down her face.

"You'll do anything to make sure your hands are clean," she said angrily. "You'll make sure the blame is placed elsewhere. Because that's what you did to Jaya and her family. Jaya was the first woman to get a head officer to consider her case against you. So you forced her son to swallow a bottle of her aspirin so that it looked like a suicide as he bled to death. That's what you did to Reina and her family. You turned

Reina's car engine on in her garage so that everyone in her house who knew you were the rapist responsible for her pregnancy suffocated from carbon monoxide. That's what you did to Neha and Madhuri. Those girls built a strong case against you. A case that would have stopped you and made you rot in prison. Instead of arresting those two suspects responsible for that school teacher's death, you contracted them to kill Neha and Madhuri with the promise of freedom by destroying the evidence against them along with the case that had been built against you," said Mandira as she shook the gun in her hand in frustration.

Arman put his hands up, presenting to the surrounding officers that he was surrendering.

"Put your gun down Mandira! He is surrendering. We will make sure he is arrested," yelled the officer.

Tears continued to fall down Mandira's face. I could see her swallow as she struggled to speak about what she had known all this time. What she had been trying to tell everyone and prove to everyone all this time.

"And that's what you did to Nima," she said after a brief pause. "She tried to kill you. She came to you to kill you. For all of the women who have become your victims. And you used her gun to try to shoot her dead after you raped her. And you planted the bombs in the hospital just to make sure that nothing could be traced back to you and that no one who might try to connect things could find you," she said with frustration.

Mandira looked at the officers surrounding the room.

"Put your guns down," she sternly told them.

Initially, everyone remained still. But soon, many women officers and a few of the men rested their guns on the ground. And as those officers rested their guns, many others joined in and even turned around, having their backs face Mandira so that they would not be considered witnesses for Arman's murder. Even more surprisingly, the officers who helped Arman cover his crimes also rested their guns and turned around.

In minutes, almost every officer turned their back to face the walls behind them and rested their gun on the floor.

But there were a few women who didn't turn around. Those were the victims of Arman. Though their guns were down, their eyes were not. They watched and waited to see what would become of Arman, seeing themselves in Mandira's shoes.

"Hey! You can't do this!" yelled Arman at the other officers. "Mandira - put your gun down! This is illegal! You can't kill a defenseless man!" he shouted.

"You don't deserve to rot in prison Arman. You deserve to rot in hell."

She raised her gun a little higher, aiming it at Arman's forehead.

"It's time to start getting our justice. God knows we deserve it," she said softly.

She pulled the trigger, killing Arman immediately. As his body collapsed to the ground, Mandira collapsed to her knees. I reached for her, catching her just before her head hit the floor and lifting her head to rest on my shoulder.

"Madhu's in the basement," she moaned in pain. "Make sure he's okay."

One of the fellow officers heard her and headed down into the basement along with some other officers.

I put my hand on Mandira's head, trying to move the hair from her face and comforting her as she rested on my shoulder. I could tell she was in so much pain. You could hear it in every breath she took.

"Is Kabir okay?" she asked as her eyes began to close.

"Hey Mandira - stay with me," I said as I slightly shook her. "Kabir's at the station - I'll make sure he's safe. He's the one that led us to you."

I could see her suddenly smile.

"That's my Kabir," she said.

Chapter 15

The scent of fresh flowers filled the Saturday morning market. Street vendors were bustling about and the honking horns of cars and buses could be heard in the near distance. The sizzling of oil blended with the sounds of chai being poured. Kabir and I were out looking for flowers for Meera's final rites as Mandira cared for Madhu at home.

While walking through the aisles of assorted flowers, I noticed how Kabir's injuries were slowly starting to heal. I gave him a black eye and reversed a lot of the care Mandira had put into him when our department got a hold of him. Now, only a slightly purple-black hue remained under his eye along with a couple of scratches on his face.

"Kabir - I am truly sorry for what I did to you," I said to him as I stopped picking flowers for a second. "I should have never hit you the way that I-"

"Don't be sorry Jamal. I'll be alright," he said with assurance and sincerity.

"But I must apologize - you didn't deserve that," I told him.

He smiled gently as he was selecting flowers from various assortments.

"A few days ago, Mandira and I stopped by Thomas Uncle's home," he said as he put some flowers into his basket.

"Thomas Uncle?" I asked, not knowing who he was referring to.

"He's a security guard at the hospital that Rhea's at right now. Mandira wanted to visit him and apologize for shooting him in the leg that night we ran out of there," he smiled. "I didn't even see him get shot, but Mandira said she was sure she had at least grazed him with a bullet and wanted to see him," he shook his head, admiring Mandira's kindness. "When we got to his house, he was sitting out on his terrace drinking a cup of chai. When he saw us, he quickly got up and welcomed us. He had a cane and was limping as he approached us, but he wasn't upset at all," said Kabir with a surprised laughter.

"By the time we had arrived, everything about what had happened had been cleared up on the news. And as Mandira and I tried to apologize, he told us not to. He said he would have done the same thing had he been in our shoes. And as we offered to pay for his medical bills, he gave the money back, saying that he was saved from the debt of killing an innocent man because of how Mandira responded that night. Thomas Uncle even said with a laugh, 'My doctor told me I'll be back to my usual self in a couple of weeks. And anyways, I got a few more days off work to spend time with my wife,' as he nudged my shoulder," smiled Kabir.

"So I'm going to pull a Thomas Uncle and say don't apologize. You were protecting your sister. That needs no apology. I would have done the same thing had I been in your shoes Jamal."

I could feel the tenseness in my shoulders release. I had felt so bad about what I had done to him. And Kabir was a great man - someone who would treat Mandira with the love and respect she deserved. I hoped that he would be in our lives for a long time.

"And thank you for protecting her," I said to Kabir. "You both make a really good team."

"She saved my life. I really love that girl. I really really do," he said as he ran his fingers across the petals of fresh red roses.

"And she really loves you. She really really does," I said with a smile.

His smile widened, and he quickly added the red roses to his basket.

"Were you able to get any updates about Rhea?" asked Kabir.

"In a couple of weeks, once the hospital gets through its last set of paperwork, they'll release her," I told him. "I was talking to Maria and she said the corporate side of the hospital is making the process a little more difficult because of the liabilities involved, especially since Rhea doesn't seem to have any living relatives."

"Hopefully, we'll be able to do her final rites soon. That's the least we could do for her," said Kabir regretfully.

"I hope so too."

We continued packing flowers into our baskets, making sure that we were selecting the best ones for Meera. Unfortunately…regretfully, it was the most we could do.

***

As I walked towards Mandira, she was holding one of the flowers we had picked out yesterday, staring into the distance. As she looked towards the river, there was sorrow on her face, but even in that sorrow, she was so beautiful. As the rising sun's beams began to reach her white churidar, I couldn't help but think that she looked like an angel.

"You guys did a great job picking these flowers. They're beautiful Kabir," she said, looking down at the flower in her hand.

I sat down beside her.

"The vendor suggested the ones that his daughter liked the most - those were the ones we picked," I told her.

She gently stroked the fragile petals.

"How are you feeling?" I asked her as I gently put my hand on her back.

"Not my best," she said, taking a deep breath and looking towards the river.

"Looking at all these preparations for Meera's rites, I can't help but think how this story could have been different for her," she said as she turned to look at me. "My mind just keeps on reliving what happened when I was with Arbazz and Arman and sometimes I feel trapped in my own thoughts and in those horrible memories. Sometimes, I wake up at night, sweating and panicked, only to realize it was a nightmare that went from being real to feeling real all the time."

Her voice became tense. She returned her glance to the flower in her hand, shaking her head in regret.

"Meera couldn't escape that nightmare. Neither could Rhea. Nor Nima. The list can go on and on. Their stories ended without them. Their voices left unheard." Her voice became coarse as she held back her tears. I reached out and held her hands in mine. I could feel the helplessness in her touch.

"But their stories won't be forgotten. Their voices will be heard," she said confidently.

Mandira gripped my hand tighter. The helplessness in her touch was dimming.

"We'll make sure of it," I assured her.

***

Walking out into the river's waters, there was both coolness and warmth. The warmth of the sun's rays and the coolness of the water's ripples as it bounced off my churidar. The skies were clear...as clear as the day had been quiet. Madhu had been standing out in the river, waist deep, for the past few minutes, staring out into the distance. As Kabir and I caught up to him, we saw how tightly he held on to his sister's ashes.

"I never thought I would be doing my sister's final rites," he said sorrowfully. "This is not how our story is supposed to end."

Kabir and I stood in silence behind Madhu. Briefly, our sorrowed eyes met in the silence. We had no words for Madhu. No way to ease his sorrow. Only time had that power.

"I'm going to make you proud Meera," he said as he held on to Meera's necklace that was wrapped around his neck.

As Madhu immersed Meera's ashes, his tears added to the depths of the waters. Kabir and I, standing beside him, put our arms around him. And out of nowhere, rain began to pour. The sun was still out, and its rays could still be seen, gleaming through the raindrops.

Madhu reached into his pocket, pulling out his necklace - the one I had seen around Meera's neck the night I found her. He gently folded it in the palm of his hand and tossed it into the water.

"I'm going to make you proud," he said again.

We watched, silently, as that necklace disappeared into the river.

Storytelling...A Passion with Purpose

A Note from the Author

Every year, millions of women and children are trafficked across the globe. Many of those voices go unheard or are forgotten.

In many cases, girls are especially likely to lose access to opportunities that can help protect them, such as their education, because of poverty, gender bias, forced child marriage, and expectations to fulfill domestic duties.

I wrote this book with the hope of being able to help change this story.

As a step towards making that difference, 100% of my profits from your purchase of this book will go towards funding the education of girls in India who face challenges in obtaining that education. Their voices deserve to be heard. Their stories should not be forgotten.

Through this initiative, my hope is that we can help them start a new chapter in their stories.

Thank you for taking this first step with me.

Made in the USA
Columbia, SC
14 February 2019